RELATIVISM
IN
CONTEMPORARY
CHRISTIAN ETHICS

RELATIVISM IN CONTEMPORARY CHRISTIAN ETHICS

Millard J. Erickson

BAKER BOOK HOUSE
Grand Rapids, Michigan

ISBN: 0-8010-3315-2

Printed in the United States of America

To the memory of my parents,
Andrew O. Erickson (1880-1970)
and
Ida C. Erickson (1888-1970),
who first taught me about right and wrong

Contents

CHAPTER FIVE
AN ALTERNATIVE APPROACH *129*

Preface

Our day has an intensely ethical orientation. The widespread concern of young people over issues such as war and peace, racial injustice, pollution of the environment, and the population explosion seems to betoken a virtual intoxication with the ethical.

Despite this, however, there is less certainty about the conclusions that should be drawn with respect to these issues. Conflicting answers, based upon differing approaches and methodologies, are manifest. The now-familiar "generation gap" has parallels here. Some seek to resolve the issues by appealing to fixed rules or laws of right and wrong. Others adopt a more flexible stance, willing to alter patterns and procedures according to the particular situation. To the former group of persons, the latter approach seems to permit virtually anything under certain circumstances. The latter type of person, on the other hand, considers the first ethical method to be rigid, harsh, and oversimplified—in a word: legalistic. How we begin will often determine or at least largely predispose how and where we finish on a particular problem. This, then, becomes the difficulty: how to settle upon a method for deciding ethical questions.

My interest in the subject dates back to the summer of 1966, when I was invited to participate in a discussion of Joseph Fletcher's book *Situation Ethics* on a television station in Chicago. The resultant thorough examination of Fletcher's thought and the considerable body of literature that has grown up about it led me to feel that I, also, should attempt to make a contribution to the subject. The real question, as I saw it, is whether there are any permanent guides to ethical decision that can be confidently appealed to in making those decisions, or whether everything depends upon the specific situation for ethical decision. Because these issues were sharply focused and widely publicized in the situationism of Fletcher and John A. T. Robinson, their thought will receive heaviest attention. The later developments, however, also deserve special attention.

The treatment will begin with an examination of the general cultural influences contributing to relativism in ethics. Then a typical contemporary form of relativism—situation ethics—will be scrutinized. Following this, the treatment of several problem areas, both by the situationists and by later advocates of ethical relativism, will be examined. This will be followed by an extended evaluation of relative ethics, both positive and negative. Finally, an attempt will be made to sketch at least an outline of a responsible alternative methodology.

Many persons have been of assistance to me in the preparation of this volume. Several of my former colleagues at Wheaton College read portions of the opening chapter and offered suggestions in their particular fields of expertise: Joseph Spradley, physics; Robert Brabenec, mathematics; George Jennings, anthropology; Samuel Schultz, Old Testament; and Steven Barabas, New Testament. Typing was done by Miss Sue Osborn, Mrs. Eileen Voth, and Mrs. Nikki Daniels. My wife, Virginia, offered suggestions and encouraged me in the task. The responsibility for all shortcomings of the manuscript, however, is ultimately mine.

Millard J. Erickson
New Brighton, Minnesota

Introduction

The last few years have proved ethically disturbing to many a layman. Morally sensitive, he has had to grapple with many significant issues: the war in Vietnam, business integrity, birth control, racial justice, and sexual morality. He asked the traditional questions. What is right and what is wrong? What are the rules that will give me the answers to such questions? And, granted a knowledge of rules, how do I know which apply? In addition to his own dilemmas, he faced the familiar "generation gap" problem. His children viewed the issues quite differently than he did.

For the layman, the problem reached a peak in the middle 1960s. What had been discussed in scholarly circles for some time came to popular attention in a movement known as "situation ethics." The writings of Joseph Fletcher and John A. T. Robinson were widely read and discussed in church circles. Situation ethics became a household word as sermons and articles sought to expound and evaluate it, usually from a negative perspective.

The Christian now found his already difficult problem considerably more complicated than before. In his search for the right rules, he was told that there are no rules, or more correctly, that there is only one rule: "Act in the most loving way." On this basis, nothing is inherently good except love. Nothing is inherently bad, except indifference. The question, "Is it right to . . . ?" is always answered the same way: "It all depends . . . upon whether that is the most loving thing to do." All of the familiar rules, laws, and standards, which he had been taught and had faithfully attempted to follow, now appeared to have been replaced by one commandment: "Love!"

Gradually the furor over situation ethics diminished. This was not because the problems had been resolved, but rather, because what was a somewhat faddish phenomenon was fading. Yet the issues that were involved in the controversy are very much alive. The ethically concerned person must still grapple with the question: Is this right, everywhere and always? And there is still a group that vehemently insists that the answer to this question must always be: "It all depends." It appears now that the popular occurrence of situationism was but a single wave of a continuing movement of relativism. Some ethical thrusts since about 1968 or 1969 have narrowed the thrust of situationism and carried certain specific emphases to their logical conclusions. Nonetheless, the same basic conception of relativism is still present.

New developments in ethics are in the very nature of things of immense importance, because they potentially affect every man. Not everyone is a physicist, a sociologist, or a mathematician. Every human being existing in society, however, necessarily engages in ethical activity. Thus, he is not removed from the topics that the ethicist discusses. Partly because of this and partly because it has been given expression in the vernacular, situation ethics has made a widespread impact on the general public.

This writer is convinced that there is need for a thorough analysis of the ethical relativism in contemporary Christian ethics. This must begin with an understanding of the entire cultural mold of the twentieth century. This will involve first a study of several developments in culture that nullified the conception of absolute notions in several disciplines. It will also take us into a study of some theological trends that tended to undercut belief in the Bible as an authority for theology and ethics. These two sets of developments, cultural and theological, will help clarify the way in which the mood has been set for the relativizing of Christian ethics.

A look will then be taken at the form and nature of ethical relativism. The example will be situation ethics, particularly the methodology of Joseph Fletcher. The major themes of this ethical methodology will be analyzed, along with some examination of the presuppositions that underlie it. This will be followed by the application of the relative methodology to several contemporary ethical issues. We will see something of the positions of the classical situationists, Fletcher and Robinson, and in greater depth, the later development of consequentialism. Among the issues examined will be several facets of current thinking on problems of sexuality.

In these chapters, the aim will be to understand what the men are saying, rather than to criticize them. In the process, however, the logical structure, presuppositions, and conclusions of the arguments will be scrutinized. This will inevitably involve some appraisal of their thinking. The fourth chapter, however, is where the direct and extended criticism will be conducted. This will be attempted both in terms of weaknesses and positive contributions. Finally an attempt will be made to sketch at least the outline of an alternative treatment.

The most crucial issue raised by these ethical methodologies is, as this writer sees it, the problem of objectivity in ethical judgments.

A key question is this: Given a situation, however carefully defined and prescribed it may be, is there for the person in that situation some course of action which is the right and good thing to do, or is this a matter of individual preference or taste? And if one grants the former, what makes one course of action the right one in this case, and wrong in another? Further, what is the means of determining right or wrong, and how is such a judgment verified? And this will lead us to the basic question of ethics: what ought I to do?

1

Cultural Backgrounds of Ethical Relativism

As cloistered as theology is sometimes pictured, it seldom functions in complete isolation from culture. Positively or negatively, consciously or unintentionally, theological systems are influenced by the milieu in which they exist. To understand such a movement, one must begin by understanding the influences, whether general or specific, that have borne upon it.

It is the thesis of this chapter that contemporary ethical relativism has at least in part been prepared for by a number of influences undermining the belief in common-sense absolutes. The first three developments have been in areas of general culture, exerting an indirect influence upon ethical theory. The next three are theological in nature, thus producing a more direct impact. The last theological influence discussed (existentialism) is of broad cultural impact. This chapter will aim at delineating and describing several of these cultural and theological developments.

RELATIVITY THEORY IN PHYSICS

In many ways the nineteenth-century view of space and time represented a systematization of the common-sense view, a systematization developed by Sir Isaac Newton.

Newton said that he would make no attempt to define space, time, place, and motion, since these were words well known to everybody. He did, however, find it necessary to distinguish between absolute and relative varieties of each.

1

Absolute or true time, he said, "of itself and by its own nature, flows uniformly on, without regard to anything external. It is also called duration." Relative time, on the other hand, "is some sensible and external measure of absolute time (duration), estimated by the motions of bodies, whether accurate or inequable, and is commonly employed in place of true time; as an hour, a day, a month a year."[1]

Similarly, Newton distinguished absolute and relative space. "Absolute space," he said, "in its own nature and without regard to anything external, always remains similar and immovable. Relative space is some movable dimension or measure of absolute space, which our senses determine by its position with respect to other bodies, and which is commonly taken for immovable (absolute) space. . . ."[2]

In each of these descriptions, Newton appeals to a concept that goes beyond our experience. In large part, it depends upon assuming an identity between our common-sense experience and "what really is." Common sense suggests an absoluteness of space, time, and motion. The earth, for instance, seems to be fixed in position, and many objects on it appear to be permanently attached to their present locations. Thus, other objects can be described in terms of these fixed positions.

Late in the nineteenth century, voices were raised protesting that the concept of absolute space is meaningless. The only way we have of judging size is by comparing the object to be measured with the size of something else. This is vividly illustrated by the story of Joe and Moe.

Joe and Moe were two sailors who were washed up on an uninhabited island. One day several years later, Joe found a bottle that had washed up on the shore. It was one of the new king-sized bottles of Coca-cola. Upon identifying it as a

---

1. Ernst Mach, "Newton's Views of Time, Space, and Motion," *Readings in the Philosophy of Science*, ed. Herbert Feigl and May Brodbeck (New York: Appleton-Century-Crofts, 1953), p. 165.

2. Ibid.

Coke, Joe turned pale and called to Moe: "Hey, Moe! We've shrunk!"[3]

Jules Henri Poincaré expressed the point in a more inclusive fashion. Suppose, said Poincaré, that while you were asleep during the night, everything, absolutely everything, became a thousand times larger than it was before. You would not notice the difference. There would be no experiment that could be performed to detect such a change. There would be no standard to which to compare, for even the standards would be changed. In fact, said Poincaré, it would be meaningless even to talk about anything being "larger" than it formerly was. Since "larger" is a comparative term and since the standard (its former size) no longer exists, there is no point in such a statement.[4]

This is similarly true of time. If suddenly all processes were either speeded up to twice their normal speed or slowed down to half the pace at which they had previously moved, there would be no noticeable difference.

For Newton, space had a very real status. He thought of it as a fixed frame of reference to which the movements and gyrations of the various celestial bodies could be related in terms of absolute motion. Space was a physical reality, stationary and immovable.

As the wave theory of light developed, scientists found it necessary to attribute certain mechanical properties to empty space—in fact, to regard it as some kind of substance. The physicists of the nineteenth century reasoned that if the waves of the sea move while supported on the water and sound waves are transmitted through air, then since light consists of waves, there must also be some medium through which these waves travel. Experiments showed that, unlike sound, light can travel in a vacuum, thus eliminating air as the possible medium. Scientists then posited a hypothetical substance called "ether" that must pervade all space and

---

3. Martin Gardner, *Relativity for the Million* (New York: Macmillan Co., 1962), p. 3.

4. Ibid., pp. 4-5.

matter. In connection with tests for the existence of ether, certain discoveries were made that led to even more revolutionary conceptions—in particular, to the special theory of relativity.

Among those who wanted experimental evidence of the existence of ether was a young naval officer named Albert Michelson. While studying physics at the University of Berlin during a leave of absence, he performed a rather crude experiment. To his amazement, he could detect no difference in the speed with which light traveled back and forth in any direction of the compass. Later he resigned his commission and became professor of physics at Case School of Applied Science in Cleveland. He soon became a good friend of Edward Morley, who taught chemistry at nearby Western Reserve University. One of the factors drawing the two men together was a common interest in testing the existence of ether. They carefully devised a more elaborate and precise apparatus to detect whether there was any impedence of the speed of light when *flowing parallel* to the ether wind (caused by the rotation of the earth in a static ether field), as contrasted with a beam of light *sent across* the ether wind. Whereas the light should be accelerated when traveling with the wind, this gain is not as great as the loss incurred by bucking the wind after being reflected in the apparatus. Thus, the light traveling parallel to the ether wind should take longer to travel a given distance than light traveling the same distance perpendicular to the wind. When Michelson and Morley employed their device, called an "interferometer," no difference could be detected. They were greatly disappointed, but the scientific world was astonished. The experiment was repeated several times by these men and others. The results were always equally negative.[5]

A real paradox was evidently present. Since the velocity of the earth as it rotated is approximately one thousand miles per hour, there should have been some noticeable difference.

---

5. Ibid., pp. 20-21.

Either, therefore, there was no ether or the earth did not move. To some physicists, the latter alternative seemed almost easier to hold. A third possibility was that the earth pulled its ether with it like an envelope. This, however, had to be rejected as a result of another experiment performed by Michelson.

It remained for a young patent clerk named Albert Einstein to resolve the dilemma and formulate a scientific breakthrough. He saw a conflict between two conceptions that he held. One was the constant speed of light, which had been determined to be 186,284 miles per second. The other was the addition of velocities.

The addition of velocities can be simply illustrated. Imagine a man walking back and forth on the deck of a ship. The ship is moving through the sea at a speed of 12 miles per hour. If the man walks at a speed of 3 miles per hour, and also walks forward on the deck, his speed relative to the sea is 15 miles per hour. When he walks aft, his speed relative to the sea is 9 miles per hour.

Similarly, picture a train moving down a track at a speed of 100 miles per hour. Ahead of it, along the track, a bell is ringing at a railroad crossing, sending out sound waves at the rate of 750 miles per hour. As the train approaches the bell, the speed of the sound waves relative to the train is 850 miles per hour. As the locomotive passes the bell and continues on down the track, the speed of the sound relative to the locomotive is 650 miles per hour. This is simple arithmetic.

One would expect that the same additions and subtractions would apply to the velocity of light. Light travels at the rate of 186,248 miles per second. Picture a rocket traveling at 18,000 miles per hour, or 5 miles per second. If the principle of addition of velocities holds true, then when the rocket ship travels toward a light source, the light should be found to be approaching at the rate of 186,289 miles per second. When the ship heads directly away, the light should overtake it at a speed of 186,279 miles per second. Yet, to the amazement of all scientists concerned, no such differences could be detected. Regardless of the speed and direction of the observation, the speed of light always remains exactly 186,284 miles per second.[6]

What could be the solution to this dilemma? Hendrik A. Lorentz and George F. Fitzgerald had suggested a solution to the ether problem that Einstein also propounded, but in a different way. If velocity is distance divided by time, then it would be possible for the speed of light to be measured as constant by all observers, regardless of the speed and direction of movement, provided the distance and time do not remain constant.

Here was a major breakthrough. As the speed of an object relative to a fixed observer increases, the lengths in the direction of the movement decrease, and all movement of a periodic sort becomes slower. Watches, hearts, and inhalation are all retarded.

Suppose a stationary observer is holding a yardstick horizontally. A rocket ship zooms past at 90 percent of the speed of light, or 167,656 miles per second, with a yardstick attached to its exterior. If the observer were able to compare the two yardsticks as they are juxtaposed, or had a camera with a sufficiently rapid shutter to be able to photograph both yardsticks simultaneously, the moving one would be seen as only half the length of the stationary stick. The relationship, however, is reciprocal. To an observer in the rocket ship, the other stick would appear to be half as long as his. The reason for the reciprocity is that motion is relative. One could as well say that the yardstick on the earth is moving by choosing the rocket ship rather than the earth as the frame of reference.

What is true of space is also true of time. To the observer on the ship, the movement of persons on the earth would seem to be in slow motion, at approximately half the normal speed. Again the relationship would be reciprocal.[7]

––––––––

6. Lincoln Barnett, *The Universe and Dr. Einstein* (New York: New American Library, 1952), pp. 49-60.

7. Gardner, *Relativity for the Million*, pp. 45-47.

The above instances involve constant velocity of the objects relative to one another. When, however, change in velocity, or acceleration, is introduced, certain interesting phenomena occur. Suppose that a man aged thirty left the earth in a space ship, leaving his twin brother behind. The ship accelerates to 167,656 miles per second and travels at that speed for a period of time during which on the earth forty years elapsed. He then returns to the earth, decelerates, and lands. His twin brother greets him as he disembarks. The earthly twin is now a seventy-year-old man. The space traveler, however, is physically and in every other respect, the equivalent of a fifty-year-old. His watch has slowed up to where it has only ticked off twenty years, and his heart, which like the watch is a periodic device, has beaten only half the number of times that it would have had he remained on earth. He has lived half as fast as his earth-twin and has consequently aged only half as fast.[8]

NON-EUCLIDEAN GEOMETRIES

A second and closely related area of the decline of the self-evident was in mathematics. Mathematics had seemed to be the model of certainty and indubitable truth. This was particularly the case with geometry.

The conclusions of geometry presuppose certain premises. These premises generally were treated in one of two ways. They might be considered to be self-evident and therefore proof is both impossible and unnecessary. On the other hand, they could be regarded as justifiable by some other proposition. It is impractical to go back infinitely, however, in the search for certainty. Consequently, geometry, like other deductive sciences, must rest on a certain number of undemonstrable axioms, or postulates.

These axioms are of two types, generic and specific. The generic axioms are held in common by geometry and other sciences. These include such items as "things equal to the same thing are equal to each other."

---

8. Ibid., pp. 117-118.

The specific axioms are those peculiar to geometry. Three of these are usually stated:

1. Through two points can pass only one straight line.
2. The straight line is the shortest distance between two points.
3. Through a given point there is not more than one parallel line to a given straight line.[9]

The third of the above propositions, known as the "fifth postulate," has received particular attention. It is sometimes referred to as "Euclid's postulate." Euclid, who lived about 300 B.C., wrote a book entitled *Elements*, which became the standard for geometry for many centuries. His proofs rested upon these specific axioms as well as several general axioms.

The second of these could be deduced from the other two as well as several others that are implicitly assumed without being explicitly enunciated. Innumerable attempts were made to prove Euclid's postulate from the other postulates.[10]

Proclus (A.D. 410-485) made one of the first serious attempts at this proof. He observed that this postulate seems to be different from the others and quite simple (a prime criterion of self-evidence). This, however, does not seem to be self-evident, and therefore an attempt ought to be made to prove it. Ptolemy (second century A.D.) had also attempted to prove this postulate. Although they succeeded, they did so only by making additional assumptions. Various substitutes were attempted for Euclid's postulate. Always the result was the same, however. Still, it was difficult to conceive of a geometry without Euclid's postulate, since upon this depended familiar conceptions such as that the sum of the angles of a triangle equals 180 degrees.[11]

---

9. Henri Poincaré, "Non-Euclidean Geometries and the Non-Euclidean World," *Readings in the Philosophy of Science*, ed. Herbert Feigl and May Brodbeck (New York: Appleton-Century-Crofts, 1953), p. 171.

10. Ibid.

11. Roberto Bonola, *Non-Euclidean Geometry* (New York: Dover Publications, 1955), pp. 1-21.

About 1830, however, a negative test was proposed. Two men, János Bolyai and Nikolai Lobachevski, independently and simultaneously proposed this. If it is the case that Euclid's postulate can be deduced from the other axioms, then if one denies this postulate and admits the other axioms, contradictory consequences ought to follow. It would be impossible to construct a coherent geometry on such consequences. Since coherence and consistency (or the absence of self-contradiction) are essentially criteria of truth in deductive systems, this seemed like an excellent indirect test of Euclid's postulate.[12]

What Lobachevski thus proceeded to do was to deny Euclid's postulate.[13] He initially assumed that through a given point two lines can be drawn parallel to a given straight line. He retained all of Euclid's other axioms, however. From these hypotheses, Lobachevski developed a geometry. Rather than encountering contradiction, he was able to construct a geometry as coherent and logical as Euclid's.

There are of course some theorems in Lobachevski's system quite different from the customary one. Here, for example, the sum of the angles of a triangle is always less than two right angles, the discrepancy between this sum and 180 degrees being proportional to the surface of the triangle. It is also impossible to construct a figure similar to a given figure, but of different dimensions. The disproof of the dependence of Euclid's postulate upon the other axioms appears to be complete. Since a self-consistent geometry has been constructed based upon A, B, C, D, and ~E, it is evident that E cannot be implied by A, B, C, D.

Another and opposite type of non-Euclidean geometry was propounded by G. F. B. Riemann in 1850.[14] He also

12. Poincaré, "Non-Euclidean Geometries and the Non-Euclidean World," p. 171.

13. Bonola, *Non-Euclidean Geometry*.

14. Poincaré, "Non-Euclidean Geometries and the Non-Euclidean World," pp. 172-173.

denied the fifth postulate, assuming rather that through a given point, no lines parallel to a given straight line can be drawn. His geometry departs more radically from Euclid's than do Lobachevski's and Bolyai's, however. In addition to the fifth postulate, Riemann also denied Euclid's second, namely that a given straight line can be extended indefinitely. Both of these were concerned with what happened if lines were extended indefinitely, which is a somewhat difficult physical task. The other postulates were retained.

Again, the result was a coherent, self-consistent geometry. Here the sum of the angles of a triangle is greater than two right angles. On a surface of positive curvature, as a sphere, the shortest distance between two points would be a great circle. Any such line drawn through a point would somewhere intersect any other straight line drawn on the surface. A triangle formed by three lines drawn on such a surface would have angles that would then equal more than 180 degrees.

The three geometries are constructed upon different types of space of constant curvature. Euclid's geometry deals with parabolic space, or space of zero curvature. Riemann's is elliptical, or positive curvature, like a sphere. It should not be confused with nonconstant curvature, like the surface of an egg, for instance. (This latter is also known as Riemannian.) The Lobachevski-Bolyai space is hyperbolic, or negative, curvature.

It thus is seen that the apparent absoluteness of Euclid's geometry is illusory. Its virtual indisputability stemmed from common sense experience of surfaces of zero curvature or surfaces differing from zero curvature by so little as to be indiscernible. Another common sense absolute had been lost.

CULTURAL RELATIVISM

When we come to the field of anthropology, we are involved in an area where the impact upon ethical thinking has been much more direct. The effect of relativistic conceptions in geometry, physics, and epistemology is only indirect and rhetorical. There is no logical connection between relativity in physics and relativism in morals. The effect of the former has been largely through the creation of a mood that was conducive to relativism in the latter as well.

Anthropology, however, deals with man and his culture. Various aspects of his behavior are studied, including his ethical life. Any tendency away from absolutism here is bound to directly affect ethical theory.

Many anthropologists have given expression to a view termed "culture relativism." One of the most consistent exponents of this school is Melville Herskovits. The sketch that follows is largely dependent upon his formulation.

Cultural relativism generally takes its beginning point from the variety of ways of life found in the human race. It is further observed that all people, when they encounter cultures differing from their own, pass judgment upon them, whether of the political organization, ethical behavior, or aesthetic production.[15]

Herskovits observes correctly that such evaluations stand or fall with the acceptance of the premises on which they are based. There is real conflict, however, among these several criteria. Conclusions drawn from one standard or definition of what is desirable will not agree with those assuming a different standard.[16]

There exist, for example, widely differing forms of organization of the primary family: monogamy and polygamy in either the form of polygyny or polyandry. Within a particular culture, its family form meets the pragmatic test. A person within that culture sees the values distinctively attaching to the form that he practices. These values, however, are not apparent to those outside. Evaluations are therefore relative to the cultural background out of which they arise.

Herskovits therefore states the principle of cultural relativism as follows: "Judgments are based on experience, and experience is interpreted by each individual in terms of

---

15. Melville J. Herskovits, *Man and His Works* (New York: Alfred A. Knopf, 1951), p. 61.

16. Ibid.

his own enculturation." The cultural conditioning to which a person has been subjected will determine what he perceives, whether in the appraisal of values or in the physical apprehension of his environment.[17]

Ernst Cassirer has observed that even the perception of space is not absolute for all persons.[18] Similarly, Herskovits tells of the foreman who drew straight lines for the native workers to follow and found that they invariably were drawn as curved. This was because the curve was as familiar and basic in their experience as the straight line is in ours.[19] This is true of other facets of human nature and human activity. John Dewey said, "Whatever are the native constituents of human nature the culture of a period and group is the determining influence in their arrangement."[20]

In the evaluation of culture, however, we encounter the mechanism known as ethnocentrism. Because one's standards have been enculturated, most persons, whether they verbalize it or not, feel that their way of life is preferable to all others. This in effect means that the criterion by which other cultures are judged is the degree of their coincidence to one's own.[21] Of course, this is usually not recognized as such. Rather than being simply one culture among many, it generally appears to be the way things really are, or ideally should be.

Ethnocentrism has positive value in making for individual adjustment and social integration. It strengthens the ego in terms of an identification with one's own group. It

----

17. Ibid., p. 63.

18. Ernst Cassirer, *An Essay on Man* (New Haven: Yale University Press, 1944), pp. 45-46.

19. Melville J. Herskovits, "Some Further Thoughts on Cultural Relativism," *American Anthropologist* 60 (1958):267-268.

20. John Dewey, *Freedom and Culture* (New York: G. P. Putnam's Sons, 1939), p. 18.

21. Herskovits, *Man and His Works*, p. 68.

also may have a detrimental effect when the standards of Euramerican culture are made the basis of programs of action for changing the cultural pattern of other groups. This sometimes has been practiced by politicians, missionaries, and others.[22]

Ethical standards, it will be seen, are now viewed as products of enculturation. Whereas some precepts have borne a seemingly absolute and undeniable force, it is seen that contradictory convictions are held with equal vehemence by persons in other cultures. That which makes a given course of action "right" is the standards of the culture within which it is practiced. Herskovits observes that all young animals provide succulent meat, yet the cultural conditioning is so strong that powerful physiological reactions such as vomiting or illness may be produced in a person who finds that he has unknowingly partaken of "forbidden" meat. The Mohammedan abhors the young pig, as we Americans (for secular rather than religious reasons) avoid puppy or colt chops.[23]

The cultural relativist, however, does not see this as destroying the objectivity of morality. Each set of norms has validity, a validity based upon the group establishing them. To attempt to erect some absolute standard is impossible. All absolutes are also derived from the culture within which they are formulated.

The cultural relativist draws a distinction between absolutes and universals. Absolutes are fixed, having no variation from one culture to another, or from epoch to epoch. There should be agreement on specifics in all cultures regarding absolutes. Universals on the other hand, are merely the least common denominators extracted inductively from the variations of phenomena around the world. Such agreement as is found here is of a rather general variety. Morality, enjoyment of beauty, and some standard of truth are

---

22. Ibid.

23. Ibid., p. 70

universally found but the specific form that they take vary widely and are, the cultural relativist argues, products of the historical experience of a particular society.[24]

Cultural relativism is not of recent origin. In its basic features it goes back at least as far as Protagorus, who maintained that morality was custom and therefore could be taught.[25] Vivas observes that the argument as usually advanced involves a movement from cultural pluralism (the fact of varying standards in different cultures) to cultural relativism. He analyzes the argument as an enthymeme as follows:

A culture determines the values acknowledged by its members. Therefore a culture determines the values its members ought to acknowledge.

The suppressed premise he sees as being:

The values determined by a culture are the values that the members of that culture ought to acknowledge.[26]

Whether this is a correct analysis of the argument and whether, if so, the argument is valid and the conclusion true, is a topic for discussion in another place. Be that as it may, the emphasis of cultural relativism has had a profound impact on the climate of contemporary ethical thinking.

HISTORICAL CRITICISM OF THE BIBLE

The absolutist tradition in Protestant Christian ethics to a large extent stemmed (as Fletcher correctly observes) from

---

24. Ibid., p. 76

25. Plato, "Protagorus," *The Dialogues of Plato*, trans. and ed. B. Jowett, Vol. 4 (New York: Random House, 1937).

26. Eliseo Vivas, "Reiterations and Second Thoughts on Cultural Relativism," *Relativism and the Study of Man*, ed. Helmut Schoeck and James W. Wiggins (Princeton, N. J.: D. Van Nostrand Co., 1961), p. 47; idem, *The Moral Life and the Ethical Life* (Chicago: University of Chicago Press, 1950), pp. 25ff.

the doctrine of verbal-plenary inspiration.[27] This view maintains that God has communicated information to man and has so influenced and guided certain men that as they wrote they recorded correctly this revelation. So complete has been God's control that the words penned by these biblical writers are the actual words that God wanted transmitted to man.

Because the commands and proscriptions in the Bible were regarded as coming from God, they carried absolute authority. If God said, "Thou shalt not commit adultery," He, having all knowledge of all situations and of their implications, could be taken literally, and this command was completely binding.

Although this view was only fully worked out explicitly in the twentieth century, it was held by the major segment of orthodox Christianity from the beginning of the movement until about the nineteenth century. To be sure, there were assaults upon the conception by secular thinkers or by left-wing movements, such as Deism. These were almost exclusively outside the church, however. With the introduction of scientific biblical criticism, this was changed.

Biblical criticism is of two types: lower and higher. These are simply terms of classification and do not carry any evaluative connotation. Lower, or textual, criticism aims at determining precisely what the wording of the original text should be. Since we do not have the original copies written by Isaiah, Moses, or Luke, and since there are a number of variations among the versions that we do have, textual criticism has necessarily become a rather highly-developed science. Chemical analysis of writing materials and ink, paleographic analysis (analysis of style of writing), and other criteria indicated comparative antiquity (and consequent relative reliability), whereas other criteria were developed to distinguish in which of two competitive readings was the type of change more likely to creep into the text, either intentionally or accidentally. Generally speaking, conservatives, such as Robertson and Kenyon, were among the most

---

27. Joseph Fletcher, *Situation Ethics* (Philadelphia: Westminster Press, 1966).

active in the advancement of this science.[28] It should be noted that the resolution of disputed passages did not really have any great effect upon Christian ethics, since for the most part no major ethical teaching passage was in question (an exception would be John 7:53–8:11).

Higher criticism, however, presented a different situation. This was the attempt to get beyond the issue of the content of the text to the meaning. It posed questions such as: "Is this account historically reliable? Did this really happen? What caused the occurrence, whatever it may actually have been?" The motivation of the higher critics needs to be correctly understood. Although they were sometimes pictured as destructive, seeking to undermine the authority of the Bible, this was not really the case. Their aim rather was simply to understand the Bible better, to find out what kind of a book it was, and to determine and understand its meaning.[29]

Note that a new conception of the Bible is operative here. For some time, historical and literary criticism had been employed in the study of nonbiblical writings. Here it had been used by Lorenzo Valla in 1440 to establish the spurious character of a document known as "The Donation of Constantine." The crucial step came when someone decided to apply to the study of the Bible the same techniques used on other writings. The assumption here was that the Bible was not necessarily different qualitatively from other books.

Higher criticism of the Bible really began with Jean Astruc (1684-1766).[30] He became particularly interested in the authority of the first five books of the Old Testament.

---

28. A. T. Robertson, *An Introduction to the Textual Criticism of the New Testament* (Garden City, N. J.: Doubleday and Co., 1925); Sir Frederic Kenyon, *Handbook to the Textual Criticism of the New Testament* (London: Macmillan & Co., 1912).

29. William Hordern, *A Layman's Guide to Protestant Theology* (New York: Macmillan Co., 1968), p. 40.

30. Gleason L. Archer, *A Survey of Old Testament Introduction* (Chicago: Moody Press, 1964), pp. 73-74.

Although he believed that Moses wrote all of these books in their entirety, he sought to determine what documents Moses might have employed in this effort. He believed he could isolate these, on the basis of criteria that have been rather strongly employed by later critics as well. Whereas higher criticism was applied to the entire Bible, its functioning can be most clearly seen in the case of the Pentateuch (Genesis–Deuteronomy). Therefore, it will be most instructive to examine the critical treatment of these books. By about 1900, the critics had reached a general consensus that the "five books of Moses" had not been written by Moses at all, but rather were a composite of the writings of several authors, material which had been compiled by one or more editors. This conclusion was reached after analyzing the text according to several criteria.[31]

The first criterion used was the divine names. Two major simple names for God are used, *Jehovah (Yahweh)* and *Elohim.* In the first thirty-four verses of Genesis, *Elohim* occurs thirty-three times. In the next forty-five verses, there are twenty instances of a compound form, *Jehovah-Elohim.* Then come ten cases of *Jehovah* in the next twenty-five verses. The question is raised as to why there is this change in vocabulary. The answer that seemed most satisfying to the higher critic was that portions of writings originated from two different authors, one of whom referred to God as *Elohim,* whereas the other knew Him as *Jehovah.* Why would a single author change the name used? This criterion was applied elsewhere, dividing the Pentateuch into two documents, J and E. As the theory was refined, E was in turn subdivided into the first and second Elohists, E and P.

A second criterion seeming to indicate a diversity of origin was the presence of doublets. There are several places in the Old Testament where it appears that duplicate accounts of the same event occur. These are of two general types.

---

31. Oswald T. Allis, *The Five Books of Moses* (Philadelphia: Presbyterian and Reformed Publishing Co., 1949), part 1.

The first type of doublet is where the Bible claims to be reporting accounts of two or more different events. For example, in Genesis 12:10-20, Abram in Egypt says that Sarai his wife is actually his sister. In Genesis 20:1-18, he does the same in Gerar in the territory of the Negeb (their names meanwhile having been changed to Abraham and Sarah). The higher critic sees here two accounts from separate sources of the same event. Because the two varied somewhat in their details, the editor presumably failed to recognize the identity of the occurrences referred to. (It is interesting that in Genesis 26:6-11, their son Isaac employs the same method, again at Gerar, and with the same king, Abimelech.) Similarly, what purport to be accounts of two expulsions of Hagar (Genesis 16 and 21:8-21) are to the critic simply variant accounts of one event.

In the other type of doublet, what the Bible reports as one account is alleged by the critic to be made up of two or more divergent accounts of the same event. There is claimed to be a double account of the Flood in Genesis 6-8. In Genesis 27:15-16, Rebekah is found to have used two means of deception upon Isaac, the use of Esau's garment being assigned to J and the skin of the goats to E. More troublesome yet is the account of Joseph's sale into slavery by his brothers in Genesis 37. This is found variously to teach 1) that his brothers sold him to the Ishmaelites at Dothan; 2) that Midianite traders sold him to the Ishmaelites at Dothan; 3) that the Midianites sold him in Egypt to Potiphar.

A final criterion of analysis was the secondary variations in diction and style. After Exodus 6:3, the divine names cease to be of help in determining sources. Other grounds become helpful, however. The vocabulary involved in Genesis 1:1-2:4a versus that of Genesis 2:4b-4:26 is an example. In the first passage, the negative particle *lo* does not appear at all; in the second, it occurs thirteen times. Death is not referred to at all in the first passage, but the verb "die" is found three times in the latter section. There are other stylistic changes found elsewhere A marked difference in tone is noticed, for example, between Isaiah 1-39 and 40-66.

In the early years of higher criticism, there was also an implicit assumption of an evolutionary development of religion. Religion, like all other aspects of culture, was believed to have developed from the simple to the more complex. Consequently, Old Testament references that had a refined and definitely monotheistic idea of God necessarily must be dated later, whereas seemingly cruder ideas would have to be assigned to an early time. This particular assumption is not present or at least not prominent in later forms of higher criticism, possibly due to the decline of general evolutionary conceptions.[32]

The usual results of the higher critical method were several. Some books of the Bible, rather than being written by the authors to whom they were traditionally attributed, were now believed to be the product of compiling the work of several writers by editors who did their work long after the events occurred. Whereas the older approach had sought to reconcile apparent discrepancies, this critical movement gave little time and effort to such harmonization. Internal contradictions were consequently found within the Bible. At numerous points, the Bible's historical references were believed to be inaccurate.

But how, one might ask, does this affect Christian ethics? Is it not a matter of indifference whether or not Moses is the author of the passage containing the Ten Commandments or some other ethical teaching? Are they not equally impressive and binding regardless?

The effect that higher criticism had upon the authority of the ethical teachings of the Bible was not immediate, but it was definite. First, it did make a difference who wrote the Pentateuch. The binding force of the Ten Commandments was a result of their being believed to be actual deliverences from God, reported by Moses. If the passage instead was written by someone else many years later (some critics even maintained that Moses could not write) the accuracy of the

---

32. John Bright, "Modern Study of Old Testament Literature," *The Bible and the Ancient Near East*, ed. G. Ernest Wright (Garden City, N. J.: Doubleday and Co., n.d.), pp. 15-18.

report was in considerable doubt. Further, if there indeed were errors and contradictions in the Bible, the verbal-plenary inspiration view appeared to be jeopardized. How could a document that contained inaccuracies be the product of an all-knowing, dependable, and all-powerful God? Finally, Jesus attributed certain sayings to men whom the higher critic now said had not written them.[33] How could this be? Either Jesus was mistaken or He had accommodated Himself to the common belief of His day. In either case, if His teaching on the authorship of the Old Testament could not be taken as authoritative, how could His ethical teachings be thus regarded?

FORM CRITICISM

Form criticism represents another stage in the study of the Bible. During much of the nineteenth century, the supernatural view of Jesus was declining. Rather than being uniquely divine, as was God the Father, He was pictured as a man like other men, but perhaps as one in whom God most fully dwelt. He was the man with the greatest God-consciousness or who most fully discovered God. The difference between Him and other men was a difference of degree, rather than of kind. This meant that the value of His teachings was not that of a divine being but rather of the sublimity of teaching of perhaps the wisest, most insightful ethical teacher who ever lived.

Under these circumstances it became very important to determine just who Jesus was, and what He actually did and taught. Consequently, nineteenth-century theologians were engaged in a "search for the historical Jesus," attempting to reconstruct His life and teachings. Historical and literary criticism was, of course, extremely important in this search.

By the beginning of the twentieth century, source criticism of the Gospels had reached a rather definitive

---

33. Edward J. Young, *Introduction to the Old Testament* (Grand Rapids: Eerdmans Publishing Co., 1949), p. 203.

position. Mark was believed to have been written first.[34] Matthew and Luke had used Mark and also another document, referred to as Q (from the German word *Quelle*, or "source"), consisting largely of sayings of Jesus. In addition, each also had access to special sources ("special Matthew" and "special Luke") containing material distinctive to his Gospel. "Special Luke" was thus believed to be the originator of the parables of the prodigal son and the good Samaritan. The Fourth Gospel was regarded as presenting such a different account as not to be considered together with the other three (the "synoptic Gospels") and as being rather unreliable.

Many critics were still uneasy with this state of affairs, however. In particular, they were concerned about the period prior to the writing of gospel records. Even the most conservative scholars dated the writing of Mark, the earliest Gospel, at least thirty years after the events, and more liberal men placed it much later. Criticism must go beyond sources and inquire as to this preliterary period.

Basically, it was agreed that the materials found in the Gospels had previously circulated as oral tradition, accounts passed by word of mouth. The aim of the form critic is to attempt to recover the earliest form of the oral tradition. The methodology of this attempt is *Formgeschichte* (literally, "form-history"), or form criticism.[35]

Beginning shortly after World War I, scholars began to scrutinize the contents of the synoptic Gospels and particularly Mark.[36] One of the first conclusions was that the

---

34. Basil Redlich, *Form Criticism* (New York: Charles Scribner's Sons, 1939), pp. 16-19.

35. George Ladd, *The New Testament and Criticism* (Grand Rapids: Eerdmans Publishing Co., 1967), p. 144.

36. For summaries of the methodology of form criticism, see: Redlich, *Form Criticism*. chap. 2; Rudolf Bultmann and Karl Kundsin, *Form Criticism* (New York: Harper & Row, 1962); Everett F. Harrison, *Introduction to the New Testament* (Grand Rapids: Eerdmans Publishing Co., 1964), pp. 146-153.

material in the synoptic Gospels had circulated as a collection of independent units; such as, stories, sayings, and anecdotes. What Mark had done was to arrange them in a historical framework. The writer is pictured as sitting down with these various units before him like a pile of unstrung pearls. The historical outline is not a part of the tradition but, rather, is supplied by the writer. The string that Mark used to connect these units is denoted by his characteristic term "immediately." The transitions are made more abruptly by Mark than by Matthew and Luke, who embellish them somewhat. They are consequently more easily discerned in his gospel than in theirs.

The attempt is then made to classify these various types of materials. Several categories are usually listed. There are, first, several types of narratives:

1. *Apothegm stories.* These are little descriptions given as background for sayings and in light of which the saying makes sense. Jesus' statement about the house of God being changed into a den of thieves, for instance, makes little sense when simply free-floating without a context. The writer gave it a setting in the story of the cleansing of the temple.

2. *Miracle stories or wonder stories.* Here there is more detail as a rule than in the apothegm story. The reason for this is that here interest is directed to the narrative for its own sake rather than being merely incidental to a saying. These stories all have a simple form that is universal, rather than being confined to the Gospels. The healing stories contain three elements: the description of the ailment; the cure, sometimes with a reference to the means used; and the effect of the cure.

3. *Stories of Jesus, other than apothegm stories and miracle stories.* There are about forty of these, apart from the birth, passion, and resurrection of Jesus.

4. *Legends.* These are accounts of extraordinary events in the lives of great religious persons, usually other than Jesus. The account of Peter's denial of Jesus and the crowing of the cock is an example.

5. *Myths describing the actions of divine beings.* They are, as Bultmann puts it, a means by which the supernatural is described in terms of the natural, or the otherworldly by the this-worldly. Examples would be the birth account of Jesus—conceived by a virgin, announced by angels, and visited by wise men who were guided to the place by a supernatural star.

There are also several classifications of sayings, as made by Rudolf Bultmann:

1. *Logia, or wisdom sayings.* The majority of Jesus' sayings have parallels in Jewish wisdom literature. Although it is possible that Jesus originated some of these, it is also possible that many Jewish proverbs were placed in His mouth by the primitive church.

2. *Prophetic and apocalyptic sayings.* In these, Jesus proclaimed the coming of the kingdom of God and gave a call to repentance.

3. *Law words and community rules.* These include Jesus' pronouncements on such matters as purity, divorce, almsgiving, prayer and fasting, discipline, and the mission of the church.

4. *"I" words.* Most of these involve the Messianic consciousness. Found here are such statements as, "I am the good shepherd" or "I am the way, the truth and the life."

5. *Parables.* These are very numerous.

Once the items in the tradition have been classified, they can then be stratified. This is to say that they can be arranged as to relative antiquity. Those found in the earlier strata of the tradition are regarded as more authentic and reliable. The assumption here is that the oral traditions found in the Gospels developed according to laws governing the development of all oral traditions.

A college student newspaper carried a cartoon in one of its issues that illustrates the development of oral tradition. In the first picture, student A is telling student B, "I saw the president of the college today, and he was wearing a red tie."

In the second picture, student B tells student C, "President X has red ties." In the third picture, student C tells student D, "President X is tied in with the Reds." Finally, D excitedly exclaims to E; "Honest, the president is an out-and-out Commie."

The point of the form critic's argument is this. The oral tradition behind the Gospels did not develop sporadically, but according to definite cause-effect laws. Given an element of the oral tradition, one can determine whether it has arisen early or late by comparing it with other oral traditions, whose history we know.

We can also stratify, says the form critic, by noting parallels between biblical materials and nonbiblical cultural influences. For example, there are roughly two types of miracles reported: the so-called healing miracles and the nature miracles. The healing miracles are typically Jewish. The nature miracles, however, are the type found in Greek thought. We know that the movement that came to be known as Christianity was initially a Jewish movement, but it came under Greek influence only after about fifteen years of its existence. Thus, the healing miracles would be regarded as relatively quite early and the nature miracles considerably later. Note that the assumption made is that similarity of material is indicative of causation or of origin.

A further assumption comes into play at this point. It is believed that in the Gospels we can find reflections of the life situation *(Sitz im Leben)* of the early church. This is to say that before the Gospels were written, the materials contained therein were being preached by the early church. The church was motivated to recall those words and deeds of Jesus that met the situations it encountered. Not only did it recall, but it may well have even placed in the mouth of Jesus, sayings that were helpful to it. Thus, the sayings of Jesus regarding rules for discipline and for the mission of the church are of rather doubtful authenticity. In fact, the sayings in which the church expressed its faith in Jesus, His work, His destiny, and His person are products of the community.

It is rather obvious that if form criticism is accepted as valid, one cannot simply quote the Gospels and say, "Jesus said. . . ." Form critics differ rather markedly in the degree of confidence they would place in the reported words of Jesus as being authentic. One of the more radical form critics is Ernst Kasemann, a post-Bultmannian, who says, "Only a few words of the Sermon on the Mount and of the conflict with the Pharisees, a number of parables and some scattered material of various kinds go back with any degree of probability to the Jesus of history himself."[37]

It should be noted, however, that one may adopt the method of form criticism and come to more conservative conclusions than this. In fact, George Ladd, himself a conservative New Testament scholar, says that when we have separated the apparent historical literary facts from the unwarranted unproven assumptions held by the extreme form critics, "we will find that at the most crucial point form criticism, in spite of many form critics, in fact supports an evangelical faith."[38]

This has not been the most frequent or the most common effect, however. Generally, the effect has been to shed doubt upon the biblical sayings as being genuine teachings, even of the man Jesus.

NONPROPOSITIONAL REVELATION

The traditional view of the Bible asserts that it is a divine revelation. God had a message that was essential for man to have. He communicated this to man, and so worked as to preserve it faithfully. Despite some recent arguments to the contrary, it appears that this is the view held by the mainstream of Christianity throughout its history.

Increasingly, difficulties were encountered with this view. Some of these have been noted above in the treatment of biblical criticism. Others arose out of what were thought to be conflicts between the Bible and natural science. New discoveries and theories in the areas of astronomy, geology,

---

37. Ernst Kasemann, *Essays on New Testament Themes* (Naperville, Ill.: A. R. Allenson, 1964).

38. Ladd, *The New Testament and Criticism*, p. 148.

biology, and anthropology appeared to contradict the traditional understanding of the Bible's teaching in those areas. Since the verbal-plenary view usually held that the Bible is completely true and free from error in all matters, this had a deleterious effect upon confidence in the Bible's authority.[39]

The response of liberalism was, for the most part, to abandon belief in the Bible as verbally inspired. Depending upon the particular thinker involved, it was seen as a record of man's religious experience, of man's discovery of God, or of God's general revelation of Himself. During World War I, however, an attempt was made, spearheaded by a Swiss pastor named Karl Barth, to take the Bible seriously and authoritatively, but not literally. This came to be known popularly as neo-orthodoxy.

The conventional approach had agreed on the nature of revelation (divinely communicated information), but had differed on its location. Protestants restricted it (as to its present existence) to the Bible. Roman Catholicism extended this to the tradition of the church. Some sects believed they were still receiving direct revelation. Neo-orthodoxy, however, changed the question. Rather than simply asking, "Where is revelation?" it raises the issue, "What is revelation?"

Neo-orthodoxy begins by asserting that revelation is personal. What God reveals is not information, not even information about Himself and certainly not information about matters of natural science. What God has revealed is *Himself*. Revelation is the full presence of God. It is in no sense reducible to a set of propositions.[40] Barth has put it thus:

> Dogmas are not *veritates a Deo formaliter revelatae*. In dogmas there speaks the Church of the past—venerable, worthy of respect, authoritative, *non sine Deo*, as befits her—but the Church; she defines (i.e. circumscribes in

---

39. William Hordern, *The Case For a New Reformation Theology* (Philadelphia: The Westminster Press, 1959), pp. 14, 56, 60.

40. John Baillie, *The Idea of Revelation in Recent Thought* (New York: Columbia University Press, 1956), p. 28.

dogmas) revealed truth, the Word of God. And thereby out of the Word of God comes the word of man, not unworthy of notice but extremely worthy of it, yet the word of man. The Word of God is above dogma as the heavens are above the earth.[41]

This means that revelation cannot be simply identified with the words of the Bible, or with the words of Jesus, even if we could be assured that the words reported were exactly what Jesus said. These are merely the means through which revelation comes. The Bible is a testimony that revelation has occurred in the past and a promise that it will occur again.

This meant that revelation was, even in biblical times, inaccessible to man's own effort. There were many who saw and heard Jesus during His ministry, but who did not meet God. A notable instance is found in John 12:28-29, where God the Father spoke from heaven and some bystanders thought an angel had spoken, whereas others said it thundered. Similarly, despite the many confused opinions about Him, Peter, speaking for the disciples, correctly identified Jesus as the Son of God, which Jesus said had not come by "flesh and blood" but by revelation from the Father (Matthew 16:13-20).[42]

To some, however, revelation did occur in conjunction with these events. The circumstances themselves did not produce the revelation, but rather were the vehicle that God used. At some point in his experience, Peter met God and saw Him in Jesus Christ. This could be described but it could not be captured. Thus, the biblical account is the record of the circumstances under which revelation occurred. It is not that revelation, per se.

Revelation is not merely past, however. As a person reads the Bible today or hears it expounded in a sermon, the experience of Peter may be repeated for him. The passage comes alive, and he is encountered and grasped and captured

------

41. Karl Barth, *The Doctrine of the Word of God, Prolegomena to Church Dogmatics*, Vol. 1, (Edinburgh: T. & T. Clark, 1936), p. 306.

42. Hordern, *The Case For a New Reformation Theology*, pp. 64-65.

by God. This, then, is revelation—the presentation of God by God Himself.

This is not some quality resident in the Bible per se. It is something that happens to the Bible. It *becomes* the Word of God, but when God withdraws Himself, the Bible is just the words of Isaiah, Mark, or Paul, who tried to give some utterance to the revelation that had come to them.[43]

Thus, the relationship of the Word of God to the Bible is paradoxical and dialectical. The answer to the question, "Is the Bible the Word of God?" is "The Bible is the Word of God—the Bible is not the Word of God." It is not the Word in the sense of some resident quality statically present. It is the Word of God in the moment in which God is using it to reveal Himself.

A story is told of Karl Barth, which, whether apocryphal or historically true, illustrates the point. Barth was preaching in a very conservative church. When he rose to speak he said, "You think this is the Word of God, don't you? Well, it isn't!" Whereupon he picked up the pulpit Bible and hurled it across the divided chancel. Then, when the effect had been fully absorbed by the audience, he went over, picked up the Bible, tenderly smoothed its pages, and explained in what sense he did consider it to be the Word of God.

Another way of putting this is to say that the neo-orthodox sees his view of revelation as dynamic rather than static. Revelation is not something that is. It is something that happens. It is not a set of propositions or black marks on a white page. It is a living, personal encounter. Part of the objection to referring to the Bible as revelation per se is that it is meaningless to refer to revelation unless it is revelation to *someone*. One of the catch phrases of neo-orthodoxy is, "no revelation without response." Like the old question of whether there is sound when a tree falls to the ground in a forest where there is no one to hear it, the neo-orthodox questions the propriety of speaking of revela-

---

43. Ibid., p. 71.

tion except in the context of the revelation coming *to* someone.[44]

Because God is a person, revelation is to be understood on the analogy of personal relationship, and cannot, consequently, be reduced to propositions. It is one thing to know about a person—his height, weight, color of hair and eyes, and personal characteristics. This, however, is not the person. It is only a police description of the person. To know him as a person is quite different. This uniqueness of the individual's reality cannot be captured within any collection of universals or classes. Knowledge of God is I-Thou knowledge, not I-It.

Nor can anyone compel God to reveal Himself. God is completely sovereign. He reveals Himself when He chooses, to whom He chooses, and by whatever means He chooses to employ. Although one can seemingly predispose himself to receive the revelation by reading the Bible, he has no guarantee that God will "speak to him," and God rather may choose to reveal Himself to a nonseeker.

An enlightened and consistent neo-orthodox pastor would therefore never preface his reading of the Scripture by saying, "We will now hear the Word of God." This would be "blasphemy," commanding God what He is to do. He would present the biblical content, hoping and praying that God would be inclined to reveal Himself.

What, then, is the status of propositions and doctrines? Brunner recognizes that these are necessary for communicating the faith. These are not the revelation, however; they *point* to revelation. They are the attempts of the biblical writers and later theologians to point to what they had experienced. We must ask of every proposition and doctrine, "Does it point to Christ?" Every doctrine is to some extent inadequate. It must constantly be criticized. If a more adequate pointer is found, it is to be substituted.[45] Because

---

44. Baillie, *The Idea of Revelation in Recent Thought*, chap. 5.

45. Emil Brunner, *Revelation and Reason* (Philadelphia: Westminster Press, 1946), pp. 118-136; *Our Faith* (New York: Charles Scribner's Sons, n. d.), p. 10.

these are regarded as growing out of revelation, William Temple has described the mood of much of the twentieth century as follows: "There is no such thing as revealed truth. There are truths of revelation: but they are not themselves directly revealed."[46]

Brunner believes that the church was overcome early with an intellectualism, generated primarily by the Hellenistic influence. The church transformed "truth as encounter" into "truth as idea." Corresponding to this, he feels, was the metamorphosis of faith from personal trust to belief in ideas. This same perversion took place again, he feels, in the second generation of the Reformation, after first-generation reformers had rediscovered the biblical view.[47]

What then is the authority of the Bible? It is not in some fixed propositions that are true in an absolute sense. These propositions are the words of fallible men. One cannot quote the Bible and equate these words with God's message in a 100 percent correlation. Billy Graham can say, "The Bible says," meaning by this, "God says"; but Barth and Brunner cannot. Rather, one must return to the encounter that is revelation, for it is that encounter alone that is really authoritative.

Finally, it should be noted that there is no external proof of revelation. One cannot erect evidential structures to prove that revelation has occurred. One cannot even offer antecedent criteria by which to judge revelation when it does happen. The revelation is self-certifying. The answer to the question, "How will I know when I fall in love?" almost invariably is, "You will just know." Similarly, this is the answer to the question, "How do I know it is God whom I am encountering (or who is encountering me)?"

What is true of the doctrinal propositions of Scripture also is true of the ethical assertions and imperatives. They are

---

46. William Temple, *Nature, Man and God* (New York: Macmillan Co., 1949), p. 316.

47. Emil Brunner, *The Philosophy of Religion* (New York: Charles Scribner's Sons, 1937), pp. 22-23, 31ff.

not divinely revealed precepts. They are ethical expressions given by men who have met God, and are attempting to convey "the divine imperative," as Brunner put it.[48] Although the obligation to obey God is absolute, the exact nature of His command is not obvious. Further, just as doctrinal propositions are authoritative to the degree that they point to Jesus Christ, so also are the ethical teachings. The neoorthodox would be more impressed by the Sermon on the Mount, given by Jesus Himself on the Mount of Olives, than by the Ten Commandments, written by Moses on Mount Sinai.

Although the neo-orthodox view of revelation is not universally held, its influence on twentieth-century theologians has been extensive. Where accepted, it has displaced the view that the ethical teachings of the Bible are to be taken as universally, absolutely, and infallibly binding.

EXISTENTIALISM

Existentialism is a movement of wide influence in our culture. Under this broad title is found an assortment of movements, persons, and ideas, so that it must be considered more a mood than a clearly isolable "school of thought."[49] It is not possible to describe it in the neat systematic way in which relativity in physics might be analyzed, for instance. At best, we can sketch briefly certain recurrent themes or motifs of existentialism that are particularly germane to ethics.

Existentialism is hostile to rationalism (in the sense of a systematic intelligible explanation of the whole of reality). Earlier philosophies looked for a pattern, a key to reality, which would serve to tie all its elements together in a meaningful fashion. Basic to this endeavor was the assumption that such a texture existed and that the philosopher's

---

48. Emil Brunner, *The Divine Imperative* (Philadelphia: Westminster Press, 1947).

49. Walter Kaufmann, *Existentialism from Dostoevsky to Sartre* (Cleveland: World Publishing Co., 1956), p. 11.

31

task was to discover it. The existentialist has given up this search because he basically does not believe that such a texture or pattern exists. He is suspicious of systems that attempt to account for everything, for these inevitably distort what they attempt to describe.[50]

Truth is found within reality when the knower examines objective data: such as physics or medicine. With respect to the really important dimensions of life, however, truth is not discovered; it is created. Values do not exist until I will them. Whether this is termed subjectivism or the priority of existence over essence, the same idea is designated: the individual, by his own free choices, brings his world into being. Something is not good because of an inherent or intrinsic quality that it possesses; it is good because (and insofar as) I will it to be good.[51]

As might be surmised from the foregoing, the existentialist makes much of the individual. Authentic existence is living as a free, self-determined individual. It means, on the one hand, not simply conforming to the conventional either because of tradition or social pressure. The individual is unique, and he must maintain that uniqueness by exercising his freedom. On the other hand, it means that the individual must accept responsibility for himself and for his situation in life. He does not excuse himself on the basis of any type of determinism—biological, psychological, sociological, or theological. He does what he does because he has chosen to do so, and for no other reason than his own freely willed decision.[52]

The themes discussed in this chapter have definite connection with ethics, and the influence has been direct and strong. If there is no pattern or interconnection within reality, then a rational ethic is scarcely possible. Rules or laws

---

50. Ibid., p. 12.

51. Jean-Paul Sartre, *Being and Nothingness*, trans. Hazel E. Barnes (New York: Philosophical Library, 1956), p. 627.

52. J. Rodman Williams, *Contemporary Existentialism and Christian Faith* (Englewood Cliffs, N. J.: Prentice-Hall, 1965), pp. 133ff.

that purport to represent what reality is and consequently to prescribe how all men ought to act are, to say the least, suspect. The emphasis upon subjectivity and upon creating values rather than discovering them is naturally more conducive to an antinomian than a legalistic type of ethic. And an emphasis upon individual uniqueness and use of personal freedom hardly is hospitable to an absolutistic ethic. The chapters that follow will reveal how this relativism has influenced contemporary ethics.

2

A Relativistic Method: Situation Ethics

Relativism in Christian ethics has taken many forms at different points in history. Even at the present time, there are a variety of expressions of this nonabsolutism. One of the most popular and influential current species is known as situation ethics. A study of its method affords us good insight into the matter in which a fairly typical ethical relativism proceeds in arriving at ethical conclusions or decisions.

Most frequently identified with the expression "situation ethics" are the names of Joseph Fletcher and John A. T. Robinson. The most complete delineation of procedure appeared in Fletcher's book *Situation Ethics*. He asserts very emphatically that situationism is a method of getting at ethical conclusions, not a system of ethical doctrines. The method, however, embodies several basic tenets that form the core of the approach. An examination of these should prove instructive in understanding how the situationist goes about his task.

Fletcher contrasts the situational method with two other approaches, between which it lies as a mean poised between two extremes. On the right is legalism. This is a form of absolutism in which a person comes to the moral decision-making situation with a prefabricated morality: a set of fixed rules, which he simply looks up in a book. Certain actions are right and certain others are wrong per se. No consideration of circumstances alters these absolutes. Murder is always wrong: abortion is invariably evil.

35

The other extreme is antinomianism. Here morality is strictly ad hoc. The antinomian enters the moral area without rules or maxims. His morality arises spontaneously, whether by some form of intuition or by a direct revelation from the Holy Spirit, or something similar.

By contrast, the situationist comes to a moral decision fully armed with all the wisdom of the past, with all of its ethical maxims and instruction. Yet he is ready to lay aside any of these, if necessary, to serve love. This is the one grand criterion: Is it the most loving thing to do? Whereas this will ordinarily mean that murder and adultery would be wrong, one cannot make a categorical judgment. Sometimes these might be the most loving thing to do. "It all depends."

The core of situationism appears most clearly in the six theses laid down by Fletcher. These had been stated briefly in his early address, which became something of a manifesto of situation ethics. Each of these, expanded and elaborated, becomes a chapter in his book *Situation Ethics*.[1] They may be stated in summary fashion as follows:

1. Only one "thing" is intrinsically good, namely, love; nothing else at all.
2. The ruling norm of Christian decision is love; nothing else.
3. Love and justice are the same, for justice is love distributed; nothing else.
4. Love wills the neighbor's good whether we like him or not.
5. Only the end justifies the means; nothing else.
6. Love's decisions are made situationally, not prescriptively.

Fletcher has given us a brief description or characterization of the role of each of these in his method:

The first one pins down the nature of value. The second reduces all values to love. The third equates love and justice. The fourth frees love from sentimentality. The

_____
1. Joseph Fletcher, *Situation Ethics* (Philadelphia: Westminster Press, 1966), pp. 18-31.

fifth states the relation between means and ends. The sixth authenticates every decision within its own context.[2]

This chapter will examine these propositions. This writer does not simply aim to state or summarize Fletcher's ideas, but to attempt to analyze certain issues that seem to underlie his position. Propositions three and four will be treated together. The treatment here should not be regarded as a substitute for reading Fletcher himself.

THE EXTRINSIC CHARACTER OF VALUE

Fletcher indicates that in his judgment the rock bottom issue of all ethics is value. He is at this point concerned with the question of its locus. Is the worth of something inherent in it? Is its worth something that it has per se, or is it contingent, or relative, to other things than itself? Basically, his position is that the only thing that is good in and of itself is love.[3]

The first issue involved is, according to Fletcher, nominalism.[4] This goes back to a dispute in medieval philosophy. The realists said that what God willed He willed because He found it to be good. Thus, preserving life is not good simply because He willed it; He willed it because it is good. The nominalists, however, such as William of Occam and Duns Scotus, said in effect that God does not discover value, He creates it by willing. Thus, murder and adultery might have been good, if God had so chosen.[5] A third possibility, not mentioned by Fletcher, is that good is good because God wills it, but that His willing is not arbitrary. It is

---

2. Ibid., p. 56.

3. Ibid., p. 57.

4. Ibid.

5. S. J. Curtis, *A Short History of Western Philosophy in the Middle Ages* (Westminster, Md.: Newman Press, 1950), p. 239.

in accord with His nature. It has an objective basis, but is not external to it.

Fletcher's point is that on the level of human value judgments, values are also nominalistic. The value does not inhere in the thing; it depends upon the person valuing it. There is a rather obvious sense in which what he is saying can be seen to be true. Which is more valuable, a quart of gasoline or a quart of water? I pay 12 cents a quart for gasoline (although I do not buy it in that quantity), and about .012 cents a quart for water. But the real value depends upon whether I am in the desert, thirsty and without transportation, or whether my car has just run out of gasoline some miles from my destination. Whether rainfall is a "good" is not inherent in the occurrence itself, but may depend upon whether I am a farmer or a weekend golfer. Thus, Fletcher moves on to say that all value is value because somebody decided it was worth something, and it all depends on the situation.[6] Note that Fletcher's nominalism is different from medieval nominalism. Here it is man, not God, who decides what is good.[7]

This means that one simply cannot say of any action that it is good or bad, right or wrong, period! What is right and good in one situation may well be wrong and evil in another. An example would be lending cash to a father who needs it for his hungry family or lending cash to a father with hungry children when he is known to be a compulsive gambler or alcoholic. Note the assumption that it is the same act in either case: lending cash to a father with hungry children. This is then an act that is variously good or bad, depending upon the situation. There are persons who would maintain that these are two different acts: lending money to a father to use to feed hungry children, or lending money to an alcoholic or chronic gambler whose children are hungry.

---

6. Fletcher, *Situation Ethics*, pp. 57-58.

7. Harmon L. Smith, review in *The Duke Divinity School Review* 31, no. 1 (Spring 1966). Reprinted in *The Situation Ethics Debate*, ed. Harvey Cox (Philadelphia: Westminster Press, 1968), p. 95.

Such persons would say that the first is inherently good and that the latter is inherently evil.

Another facet of this view is that love is a predicate.[8] Values in general must be seen as being predicates only, not properties. They do not have some independent existence or objective reality. The only "thing" that is always good, regardless of context or situation, is love. Even that is not considered to be a self-existent entity. It is merely a formal principle.

Part of the confusion that we find in Fletcher stems, I believe, from failure to discriminate among four uses of the simple verb, "to be." 1. The "is" of existence: "_____ is." 2. The "is" of identity: "Water is H_2O." 3. The "is" of inclusion: "George is a bachelor" (member of the class of unmarried males). 4. The "is" of predication: "That book is red." A Platonist, of course, would maintain that the fourth variety can be reduced to the third, since for him there is no subject to which something else is attributed. There are only existents that participate in the form of . . . (whatever be the predicate term). Seemingly in Fletcher's thinking there is a rather widespread tendency toward Platonism—reifying terms, making them substances or essences.

Love, he says, is not something we have or are. If it were a substance or a property this would be possible. Rather, love is something relational—a certain way of relating to persons. One cannot really say "I love" or "I have love," in the abstract. Love is not something with real existent status, any more than is "upside-downness." It is simply a way of characterizing some ways in which we act.[9]

There is one exception to this seeming rule. That is God. In God, love is not simply a descriptive expression. God is love (presumably in sense number 2 above). Men *do* love. That which is a predicate with respect to man is a property in God.[10]

---

8. Fletcher, *Situation Ethics*, p. 60ff.

9. Ibid., pp. 60-61.

10. Ibid., p. 62.

Apparently he is saying that love is always and everywhere good because God is love. A question that should probably be asked is whether this implies that this is the only property of God. If the statement "God is love" is indeed an identity statement, it ought to be convertible, thus: "Love is God."

The other side of this is that only one thing is intrinsically evil or bad, namely indifference. The opposite of love is not hatred, for hatred at least treats the other, the neighbor, as a *thou*, whereas indifference turns the neighbor into an *it*, a thing. The very nadir of human relations, he says, is the attitude, "I couldn't care less."[11]

This is his last summary statement: all values are only extrinsic. This places him in opposition to all views of laws and maxims (other than that one should always love) as being "objectively valid," irrespective of circumstances. It also means that there are no universals of any kind, except love.

The intrinsicalist holds that certain actions are wrong or evil in themselves. Kant, for example, taught that a lie is always wrong. Fletcher would say that lying is neither good nor bad per se. It *becomes* good or bad dependent upon whether it serves love. Thus, a lie told for a loving purpose is *good*; if it is told from an unloving motive, it is *evil*.[12] Note that he is not saying that a lie is ordinarily evil, that it is evil *unless* it is told for the sake of love. He believes that he is supported by Paul's statement in Ephesians 4:15 about "speaking the truth in love." He maintains that this is instructing us to tell the truth not for its own sake but for the sake of love.[13]

This also means that for Fletcher there is no separation between the good and the right. What is the right thing to do in a certain situation is thereby also good. The intrinsicalist recognizes the difficulty faced in some decision situations.

---

11. Ibid., pp. 63-64.

12. Ibid., p. 65.

13. Ibid.

Suppose that I am asked the location of a man by another man whom I have reason to believe intends to murder the first man. I know where he is. What should I do? The intrinsicalist would probably say that it is not good to lie, but that in this case it is the *lesser of two evils*, and therefore is right and ought to be done. Where Fletcher would differ is in saying that it is not an evil of any kind. If it is what I ought to do, it is good. He states his position in unequivocal fashion:

> Right and wrong, good and bad, are things that *happen* to what we say and do, whether they are 'veracious' or not, depending upon how much love is served in the situation. The merchant chose to do a good thing, not an excusably bad thing. Love *made* it good. *The situationist holds that whatever is the most loving thing in the situation is the right and the good thing.* It is not excusably evil, it is positively good. This is the fundamental point of the extrinsic position.[14]

There are certain practical differences that emerge from this. The intrinsicalist might well tell a lie under certain circumstances but would do so with a sense of remorse and regret. The extrinsicalist need feel no such emotion, however. It is not bad to lie if love is served; it is positively good.[15]

The point clearly has been made, and, as Fletcher indicates, it is a crucial one. Upon this, much else will follow.

LOVE ALONE AS NORMATIVE

The second tenet of situationism deals with the relationship between this command to love and other possible norms or "laws." Are there any other rules that are always to be obeyed? As has already been noted, the situationist (according to Fletcher) has only one norm. He reduces law to this single canon of love.

---

14. Ibid.

15. James M. Gustafson, "How Does Love Reign?" *The Christian Century* 83, no. 18 (May 1966): 654-655.

This is to say that love has replaced law. There is a conflict between the two, which has been resolved by elevating love. If law is followed, it is for love's sake, not vice versa.[16] Robinson sees law and love as in tension with each other, a tension that should be maintained. They are but two different ways into the same reality. Neither side should be denied.[17] Fletcher, however, is more emphatic or, as he says, adamant, in his denial of any union between the two principles.[18]

The conventional or legalist approach is that through obeying law we serve love because there is no real conflict between law and love. In Mark 12:29-31, for example, Jesus summarized the law by saying you shall love God with all your being and you shall love your neighbor. Legalists regard the summary as a compendium, the keeping of each of these many laws being implicit in the summary. The situationist, however, considers it a distillation in which the essential principle has been extracted from the many laws, eliminating the legal husks, or rubbish. Love will employ law when it seems worthwhile, but they are basically opposed.[19]

There are several lines of evidence that are offered for the rejection of legalism as a guide to conduct. These will be examined in turn.

1. There can be at most only one absolute norm. If any one principle had an absolute, inalienable right to be observed, then every other rule, should it conflict with it, would have to give way.[20] Suppose my personal code of ethical absolutes includes (1) I should never tell a lie, and (2) I should never break a promise. What then am I to do in a

---

16. Fletcher, *Situation Ethics*, pp. 69-70.

17. John A. T. Robinson, *Christian Morals Today* (Philadelphia: Westminster Press), p. 20.

18. Fletcher, *Situation Ethics*, p. 70.

19. Ibid., pp. 70-71.

20. Ibid., p. 36.

situation in which I can only keep a promise to one person by lying to another? There must indeed be one prime absolute, says the situationist, and that norm is love. The assumption, of course, is that if there are two or more norms, they will, sooner or later, inevitably conflict.

2. Jesus is seen as having denied or broken the law of His day for the sake of love or benevolent concern for His fellowmen. A prime example of this was His allowing His disciples to pluck grain on the Sabbath. He even justified this by appeal to David's act of taking the shewbread (Matthew 12:1-8). Other notable cases involved His healing on the Sabbath day. Jesus' position was that man was not made for the Sabbath, but the Sabbath (the law) was made for man.[21]

3. There are believed to be other direct teachings of Scripture that negate the practice of legalism. One of these is Paul's statement in II Corinthians 3:6 that the letter (adherence to the law) kills, but the spirit gives life.[22] Furthermore, Paul is quoted as saying in I Corinthians 6:12 that what matters is what is upbuilding, rather than what is lawful.[23]

4. The attempts to convert the moral teachings of the Bible into legalistic rules is impossible. These were simply illustrations of the meaning of divine love in certain specific situations. They cannot be generalized into a code of conduct because they fail to take into account other demands upon, and responsibilities of, the person. To some extent this is a variation of the first objection. In the Sermon on the Mount, for instance, Jesus says, "Give to everyone who asks of you," without any thought as to the stewardship of money. He commends the widow who cast all her livelihood into the treasury without concern about who would henceforth

---

21. Fletcher, *Situation Ethics*, pp. 85-86; Robinson, *Christian Morals Today*, p. 24.

22. Fletcher, *Situation Ethics*, p. 69.

23. Ibid., p. 75.

support her. The command to turn the other cheek when slapped on the first cheek would seem also to preclude any type of self-defense.[24] Fletcher seeks further to show this by a rather detailed scrutiny of the Ten Commandments.[25]

5. Still another objection to legalism is based upon its effects. Frequently, it not only expresses love imperfectly, it even militates against love. Fletcher cites a court case of a few years ago in England. The law then stated that marriage to be legal must have been validated ("consummated" by sexual union). In this case, this had not been possible because of a physical problem on the part of the husband, which was later medically corrected. A child had been born to the wife by means of A.I.H. (artificial insemination by the husband). The court, however, ruled in keeping with the law, that the child was conceived out of wedlock and was therefore illegitimate, that the wife was husbandless at the time of her son's birth, and that the father was without a son and heir even though the child was literally the physical offspring of both. This is cited as an example of what legalism does. Rather than serving human welfare, it requires that the law be satisfied, irrespective of the human consequences.[26]

6. Legalism also is rejected because its motive and purpose is to minimize obligation. This may frequently be carefully hidden, but it is there nonetheless. It indicates what one must do and no more. He is not saying that law prohibits one doing more than the minimum, simply that it does not require one to do more.

As examples of the effect of legalism, Fletcher cites cases from our society of persons simply standing by while people are attacked or other disasters occur without helping. The reason was that the law didn't require them to do so! On

---

24. Robinson, *Christian Morals Today*, pp. 27-28; Fletcher, *Situation Ethics*, p. 77.

25. Fletcher, *Situation Ethics*, pp. 71ff.

26. Ibid., pp. 78-79.

the other hand, love does not put a ceiling or a floor on obligation. It seeks the maximum good in each situation.[27]

7. Similarly, it is doubtful whether legalism's effort to *force* people to be good can succeed. Part of this is implicit in number 5 above. The law, for the most part, works toward prohibiting badness, rather than positively promoting goodness. This also, however, suggests that real goodness is not present where conduct is governed by fear of prosecution or public opinion. Sexual morality has in the past frequently been motivated by the triple terrors of infection, conception, and detection. These deterrents are now, through medicine and urbanism, largely obsolete. This, however, opens the door for genuinely moral decision, which would of course be done situationally, not legalistically. Like Gyges in Plato's *Republic*, what would one do if he could become completely invisible?[28] Add to this whatever details you might wish, and you have a situation in which a decision would be made not out of legalistic fear but out of genuine freedom. Legalism, because it does not allow for real freedom, must be rejected.

8. Finally, the situationist uses an empirical argument against the existence of universal norms. Although willing to grant hypothetically the natural law advocate's postulating the presence of right and wrong objectively in the nature of things, there is a noticeable gap between this and believing that anyone can actually determine what such absolutes may be. He says:

> No twentieth-century man of even average training will turn his back on the anthropological and psychological evidence for relativity morals. There are no "universal laws" held by all men everywhere at all times, no consensus of all men.[29]

---

27. Ibid., p. 82.

28. Plato, *The Republic*, trans. Benjamin Jowett (New York: Random House, 1937), 1:623.

29. Fletcher, *Situation Ethics*, p. 76.

Fletcher then goes on to condemn the study of nature as a means of discerning God's will in it as committing the naturalistic fallacy of deriving *ought* from *is*.[30] It should, however, be noted, as Paul Ramsey has observed, that Fletcher appears to have committed the naturalistic fallacy himself, having derived the relativity of morals (as contrasted with the pluralism of ethical behavior) from anthropological and psychological evidence.[31]

There seems to be a rather notable difference between Fletcher and Robinson. If one asks the question, "Are there any acts that invariably are expressions of love?" he is posing a semi-intrinsicalist or legalist type of question. It is not a matter of whether these are acts that are right or wrong in themselves, but whether they always embody love and *for that reason* are always right. To this question Fletcher seems to say "no." Robinson, however, says:

> There are some things of which one may say that it is so inconceivable that they could ever be an expression of love—like cruelty to children or rape—that one might say without much fear of contradiction that they are for Christians always wrong. But they are so persistently wrong *for that reason.* There is not a whole list of things which are 'sins' *per se.*[32]

In practice, however, the discrepancy is not as great as it seems. Robinson is affirming that these acts are not good per se, thus not intrinsically. And, as we shall later observe, even Fletcher is willing to say of some acts that the situationist would almost surely approve of them, i.e., consider them to be inseparably connected with love.

THE NATURE OF LOVE

It is necessary to understand the nature of this love that is to guide all moral decisions and action. The idea that

---

30. Ibid.

31. Paul Ramsey, *Deeds and Rules in Christian Ethics* (New York: Charles Scribner's Sons, 1967), p. 157n.

32. Robinson, *Christian Morals Today*, p. 16.

generally comes to mind when love is mentioned is a sort of sentimental feeling of positive liking. Fletcher is clear that this is not what he means by love.

Numerous researches have been done on the precise meanings of the various Greek words for love, probably the most exhaustive being Anders Nygren's *Apage and Eros.*[33] *Philia* is friendship love. It has a warmth of affection. *Eros* is the acquisitive love, most clearly seen in heterosexual romantic attraction but also found elsewhere. It is also characterized by emotion. It seeks the other person for the satisfaction that can come to itself. It is attracted by qualities in its object. It is motivated by desire.

Agape is different from both of these, but particularly from *Eros.* It is not caused by desire; rather, it is the cause of desire. It is not motivated or appealed to by the attractiveness of the object. It is virtually indifferent to such qualities. It does not have as its aim the extracting of value from the object, but rather the conferring of value.[34]

This type of love is not primarily a function of emotion. It is rather an active determination of the will. It is the determination to do good to certain persons in need. It is an active doing rather than a feeling. It is nonreciprocal, that is, it is extended to the deserving and the undeserving, to the appreciative and the unappreciative, and to those who return it with love and those who return hate or, worse yet, indifference.[35]

This kind of love can be commanded whereas the other two cannot. It makes no sense to say, "Love your enemy," if by this is meant a certain emotion. One simply does not decide how he will feel and then feel accordingly. Emotions are not under the control of the will. If they were, few people would feel sad and there would be considerably less

---

33. Anders Nygren, *Agape and Eros* (London: S.P.C.K., 1953).

34. Fletcher, *Situation Ethics*, p. 105.

35. Ibid., p. 106.

anger than there is. To try to produce or simulate this is to practice hypocrisy.[36]

What Fletcher is saying seems to be psychologically sound and supported. There are some persons whom, at least initially, we have great difficulty liking. The reasons may be on a conscious or an unconscious level. They may do things that conflict with our desires or they may simply have mannerisms that annoy us. There may be some things about them that remind us of someone with whom we once had an unpleasant experience. Whatever the reason, we do not find it easy or even possible to feel attracted to them.[37]

If, however, love is doing certain acts of benevolence, it can be commanded and controlled. One can grit his teeth and resolve, "I will help him." No insincerity would seem to be involved, unless effusive expression of warmth of feeling is made to accompany these acts.

Therefore for Fletcher, love must involve impartiality. An umpire may well like some good-natured ballplayers much more as individuals than he does the surly fellows. Love means, however, that he calls "balls" and "strikes" and "safe" and "out" irrespective of the persons involved. Similarly, a teacher is naturally attracted to some students more than to others. Love, however, means that he assigns grades as fairly as possible regardless of the appeal that the person has for him.

This does not mean that the love relationship is necessarily exclusive of the philic. In fact, beginning by willing and doing the other's good often leads to the feelings. This is, however, the consequence rather than the cause, and this should be clearly kept in mind.

Whereas there is much in Fletcher's analysis that seems to be sound psychologically and theologically, there are other points at which his treatment seems to be a bit naive in these respects. For example, his assumption seems to be that the effect of liking and loving is always at the conscious level.

---

36. Ibid.

37. Ibid., pp. 107-108.

Thus, while I may not feel especially favorably disposed toward another person I may resolve that I will do good to him. The very difficult problem, however, is that on the subconscious level, my dislike may overwhelm my love, affecting even my judgment of what is actually good for the other.

Nor should Fletcher's enumeration of cases of *agape* be taken uncritically. Here he seems to impute his own cultural setting, or set of presuppositions, so that anyone who performs an act that appears not to be personally self-rewarding is believed to be acting out of *agape*. Military men who in war voluntarily give their lives for their country's fortunes or for their fellow soldiers are notable cases. Yet one must ask of each case, it would seem, whether altruism was the motivating factor or whether there were less apparent reasons. For example, he includes a kamikaze pilot among those whose acts are examples of selfless, calculating concern for others.[38] The kamikaze flyers, however, believed that by giving their lives in this fashion they were guaranteeing immortality to themselves. This may have been something other than *agape*.[39]

There is a place within this picture for acting for one's own welfare. When this is done, however, it is in a different fashion than pure egoism, for a person here acts so as to be able to love others. Thus, if the United States were under bomb attack, *agape* would dictate that the president preserve his own life, but not for his own sake. Although it might superficially appear that the loving thing to do would be to assist others in need, he would ultimately do more for more people if, disregarding their predicament, he were to flee for shelter so that his special ability might be preserved and employed.[40]

---

38. Ibid., p. 110.

39. Thus, Charles Curran maintains that Fletcher has not solved the age-old problem of the relationship between *Agape* and proper love of self. Charles E. Curran, "Dialogue with Joseph Fletcher," *"The Homiletic and Pastoral Review* 67, no. 10 (July 1967): 825.

40. Fletcher, *Situation Ethics*, p. 113.

Fletcher sees the two commandments of Jesus (to love God and to love one's neighbor) as being one command. The three objects of love (God, neighbor, and self) unite love's work. As will be noticed later, Fletcher makes less of the command to love God than he does of the command to love one's neighbor, and this may well be his reasoning.

Nor does love exclude the functioning of reasoning and calculation. If it is really to work for the ultimate welfare of people, it may well have to coolly and carefully calculate the best way to achieve that end. Fletcher cites with approval the minister who did not immediately give a handout to every panhandler who came to him. The person's problem is not always solved by giving him what he directly asks for. One also has to determine what is the best use of the available resources.[41] *Agape* will not always please the person. It does not simply avoid unpleasantnesses. It does what has to be done. It may deceive. It may even make the other person angry, like the nurse who made soldiers hate her so that they would get on their feet more quickly.[42]

Love can be angry, also. Love is not simply the indulgent approach that overlooks shortcomings and wrongs. The picture that the liberal sometimes had of God as a sort of benevolent grandfather was transferred to the kind of love that man would then have in emulating God. This is not what Fletcher has in mind. Love makes judgments. It does not say "forget it"; it says rather, "forgive it."[43] Fletcher is trying to convey a picture of love as being morally responsible rather than merely liking and feeling good toward everyone. He has tapped uniquely biblical insight in so doing.

This logically connects with Fletcher's utilitarian understanding of love. Whereas he deals with this aspect prior to the chapter "Love Is Not Liking," it seems to this writer to be logically antecedent to it, growing out of the statement of

---

41. Ibid., p. 116.

42. Ibid.

43. Ibid., p. 117.

love's impartiality, nonsentimentality, and calculating character. It is a further delineation of the nature of *agape*.

Love is responsible to all of one's neighbors, his friend-neighbor, acquaintance-neighbor, stranger-neighbor, and even enemy-neighbor. This means that one does not simply respond to the needs of the neighbor who is most immediately at hand. His needs may seem to be the more vivid, and if love is seen as sentimentality, it may seem to be at variance with justice (providing what is due to all my "neighbors"). Properly seen, it is not so. Justice is simply love distributed to a large number of neighbors.[44]

Fletcher seems very concerned to remove this conflict, perhaps unduly so. It is this writer's judgment that the tension, which he attributes to many people, between love and justice may be the result of a conflict between two divergent movements or systems of thought that have influenced Fletcher in the formulation of his situationist method. These are existentialism and utilitarianism.

The symptoms of existentialism have been observed earlier. One of the prime tenets of existentialism is its individualism. It emphasizes "I-thou" relationships, and decries the losing of individuals in the crowd. Utilitarianism, on the other hand, takes as its slogan, "the greatest good for the greatest number." Fletcher definitely indicates that the love ethic must form a coalition with utilitarianism and take over this very principle from Bentham and Mill.[45] What is needed is to retain the personal, human relationship of existentialism and add to it the distributed responsibility of utilitarianism. What Fletcher seems to be asking for is (to give the expression a Southern flavor) an "I-y'all" relationship. Justice is simply a name for love, functioning in situations in which distribution is called for. Love, however, always finds that it must confront many neighbors.

---

44. Ibid., pp. 89ff.

45. Ibid., p. 95; cf. William Robert Miller, review in *The New Republic* (September 1966). Reprinted in Cox, *The Situation Ethics Debate.* p. 83.

Fletcher makes one major distinction between his approach and utilitarianism. He feels that situationism accepts the procedural principle of utilitarianism, namely, distribution of benefits, but changes the value principle from pleasure to love.[46] Actually, it would appear that utilitarianism is basically a method rather than a system, so that hedonism is not inherent in it.

Fletcher gives several illustrations of this, which emphasize that love cannot always do the maximum good to everyone, and therefore love must choose. In such situations, love calculates and seeks to help the many, not the few, regardless of how one may feel towards the persons involved. Thus, when a resident physician in a hospital emergency room decides to give the hospital's last unit of blood plasma to a young mother of three rather than to an old skid row drunk, the choice is not between "disinterested" love and justice. In choosing to serve many rather than few, justice is being served.[47]

One crucial difference between the situationist and the legalist, or intrinsicalist, emerges rather clearly in one of Fletcher's stories. During World War II, the British intelligence staff had to make a critical decision. Because they had broken the German code, they knew that if a number of women agents were sent back to Germany, they would certainly be arrested and put to death. If, however, they did not send them back, the Germans would know that the integrity of their code had been destroyed. The women were sent. Fletcher says that "legalistic casuistry could not comfort the British intelligence staff. . . . Situational casuistry could easily approve their decision."[48] The difference in mood seems definite. The intrinsicalist might well have approved what was done, but would have termed it "the lesser of two evils." With real regret and anguish, he would

---

46. Fletcher, *Situation Ethics*, pp. 95-96.

47. Ibid., p. 97.

48. Ibid., p. 98.

have allowed the women to go to their death to prevent a greater loss of life. The situationist, however, sees nothing intrinsically bad or wrong about anyone's death. If justice is served (the greatest good for the greatest number), then this can be termed "good."

Fletcher is concerned to communicate that love is not simply soft, sentimental, and indulgent. It *must* calculate as to whom to help, and in this it may sometimes seem quite hard. This is in no sense in tension with the fundamental conception of love's nature, however.

On this basis, presumably Fletcher would approve of so-called "poverty tests" for recipients of welfare. Whereas these may have a demeaning effect upon an occasional person, they help to insure more adequate benefits for a larger number of needy or worthy applicants and to prevent excessive taxation of a large number of citizens.

Fletcher would insist upon a significant distinction, between *moral* justice and *legal* justice. There is nothing inherently antithetical about the two, and ideally they ought to coincide, but sometimes they do not. In this case, it is moral justice that must be followed.[49]

One important qualification to his overall principle of enemy-love has to be made: "it is right to deal lovingly with the enemy *unless to do so hurts too many friends.*"[50] The illustrations he offers do not directly relate to this point but do give us insight into his method, nonetheless. If one can carry either DaVinci's *Mona Lisa* or a baby from a burning building, a personalist takes the baby, says Fletcher. But if the choice is between your father and a medical genius who has discovered a cure for a common fatal disease, *agape* dictates that you take the genius.[51]

Two observations should be made concerning these examples. First, the question is not merely which course will

---

49. Ibid., p. 99.

50. Ibid., p. 115.

51. Ibid.

benefit the larger number, but also the quality of the benefit must be determined. On the surface, large numbers of persons would stand to receive enjoyment from the *Mona Lisa* (although, as Fletcher notes, there are photos and copies of the painting). The life of a person is, however, presumably of much greater value than the cumulative pleasure that these many people would derive from seeing the original painting (the baby, of course, may even turn out to be another DaVinci). Second, the calculation seems to be solely consequence oriented. The question is whether greater benefit will result for more persons by removing the medical doctor than by saving the father. Any question of past obligations or responsibilities does not enter the decision. This introduces the idea that ends justify the means, nothing else.

Finally, when Fletcher says it is right to deal lovingly with the enemy unless too many friends are hurt as a result, he does not tell us how many is too many. There is no formula given for calculating precisely the relative weights and values to be assigned. This is the point of the final tenet to be considered: that love decides then and there (i.e., situationally).

It is also worth observing that Jesus falls short of Fletcher's standard. The first instance deals with the account of the anointing at Bethany (Mark 14:3-9; Matthew 26:6-13; John 12:1-8), when a woman anointed Jesus with very costly ointment. The disciples seeing this were indignant (John attributes this to Judas). Why, they said, was this ointment not sold for three hundred denarii (about sixty dollars) and given to the poor? Jesus is pictured as defending the woman on the grounds that she is preparing His body for burial and that they always have the poor with them. Fletcher feels that the real issue is between "impetuous, uncalculating, unenlightened sentimental love" on the part of the woman, and a calculating, enlightened, and utilitarian love by the disciples. (He brushes aside the motivation of personal profit through embezzlement, which John attributes to Judas.) Fletcher says, "If we take the story as it stands, Jesus was wrong and the disciples were right."[52] He observes that some have

52. Ibid., p. 97.

sought to excuse Jesus on the basis that He was really in agreement with the critics but was trying to comfort the woman by softening the blunt and harsh criticism. He does not indicate whether he accepts this explanation, but he does say, "We do not have to conclude that He ever said anything at all like, 'You always have the poor with you.' "[53] No support is offered for this assertion. Presumably it is a conclusion drawn from the application of a critical method.

Three possible interpretations could be given to Fletcher's discussion of this incident:

1. The story is to be taken as it stands, and utilitarianism, opposed by Jesus, is to be rejected.
2. The story is to remain intact and Jesus was wrong— He was subagapeic.
3. The story cannot be regarded as authentic in its given form. Consequently, there is no evidence here that Jesus fell short of utilitarian agapeic situationism.

It appears quite definite that number 1 is not what he has in mind. This leaves the choice between numbers 2 and 3, and it is difficult to determine which Fletcher adopts. It is certain, however, that for Fletcher the picture drawn of Jesus by the Gospel writers is not the standard to be adopted.

A second point of his implied criticism of Jesus is in connection with the golden rule. He notes with apparent approval a common criticism of the classic statement "Do unto others as you would have them do unto you." The criticism is that this is "self-centered, cutting its cloth according to what you want rather than what the neighbor wants." Even the suggested modification "as they would have you do unto them" is inadequate. Rather, he says, "*agape* is concerned for the neighbor, ultimately, for God's sake; certainly not for the self's, but not even for the neighbor's own sake only."[54] It would appear that, again, Jesus' statement is judged to be less adequate than Fletcher's.

---

53. Ibid.

54. Ibid., p. 117.

Even Jesus' statement of the key distillation of the law, "You shall love your neighbor as yourself," must be modified to make explicit that which is implicit. Says Fletcher:

> In all humility and in spite of any hesitations based on false piety and Biblicism, Christian ethics is under grave obligation to do some tinkering with Scripture—i.e., with translations from the Greek of the Summary. And why? Because we have to add an 's' to 'neighbor' in that distillation of the law. . . . We must sophisticate the childish notion that love is only for people one at a time.[55]

It is clear that Fletcher is no "Biblicist." He has not abstracted his love principle from the Bible, regarding it in simple, literal fashion. He has, as he indicates, voluntaristically accepted love by "positing" it, and it is the criterion by which even the Scriptures are judged.

CONSEQUENCES AS THE JUSTIFICATION OF MORAL ACTION

The situationist dictum that "only the end justifies the means" is in a sense not a separate proposition. It was implied by the idea that values (except *agape*) are extrinsic only, not intrinsic. What Fletcher is doing is deducing this. If no action has an intrinsic value, then it can only be appraised and evaluated by whether it is part of a chain in which it ultimately is a means to the good end of *agape*.

Fletcher objects violently to the principle that "the end does not justify the means." He believes that Christian ethics down through the centuries has stubbornly clung to this dictum. He seems to assume that this assertion means that a good end is not a necessary justification of a means, when he states that "use or usefulness is *irrelevant* to price" (italics added).[56] But he later seems to acknowledge that the legalist is simply claiming that it is not a sufficient justification.

---

55. Ibid., p. 91.

56. Ibid., p. 120.

On the contrary, Fletcher says that if the end does not justify the means, nothing does. Without an end or purpose in view, any action is literally meaningless, random, accidental, and pointless.[57] This goes beyond the analytic statement that "ends justify means." It is saying that all actions are means, that they must visualize some end.

Just what does Fletcher mean by saying that the end justifies the means? There are four logical possibilities:

1. A good end justifies a good means
2. Any old end justifies a good means
3. A good end justifies any old means
4. Any old end justifies any old means

Number 1 and number 2 are eliminated immediately. No value is intrinsic in any act, as we have already seen. Thus, it is meaningless to talk about means as being good or bad apart from the question of the end. Further, he explicitly rejects number 4. This apparently leaves us with number 3 as the true meaning of his statement:

> It should be plainly apparent, of course, that not any old end will justify any old means. We all assume that some ends justify some means; no situationist would make a universal of it! Being pragmatic, he always asks the price and supposes that in theory and practice everything has its price. *Everything*, please note (italics his).[58]

On this point Fletcher seems to be unusually concerned to cite scriptural support for his position. He notes that Paul twice in I Corinthians (6:12 and 10:23) says that all things are lawful, but not all things are edifying. This he believes to be a refutation of the intrinsicalist approach. It is the result to which it leads that counts.[59] Yet Paul is not necessarily identifying the lawful with the good. To be good means being lawful plus being helpful. Not everything lawful is helpful

---

57. Ibid.

58. Ibid., p. 121.

59. Ibid., p. 125.

and therefore good. He is not asserting that what is unlawful can become good by being edifying.

That this is more nearly what Paul had in mind would seem to be established by Paul's treatment in Romans 3:8 of the question, "And why not do evil that good may come?" (as well as his statement in Romans 6:1-2, which Fletcher bypasses). Fletcher feels that this passage has been used by legalists who quote it out of its context of having been made in the heat of a controversy with the antinomians.[60] Properly understood, he would say it constitutes no threat to his view.

Quoting out of context does not seem to be consistently avoided by Fletcher, who quotes from Isaiah 4:1, where the prophet foresees a day when seven women will take hold of one man. He believes this justifies polygamy in certain circumstances (i.e., when it serves a good end).[61] Yet, he seemingly fails to note that Isaiah is depicting a future scene of judgment, and in no sense condones or approves what he describes.[62]

If the means are only extrinsically good, only good when leading to good ends, so also must ends be regarded as only relatively good. All ends in turn become means to some higher end. As will be familiar by now, the only thing intrinsically good is *agape*, which is the ultimate end by which all means, some of which are intermediate ends, are justified. One must not stop with any of these ends as good in themselves but must press on to the question of whether this contributes to *agape*.[63]

The ends justification must be double edged. Not only may means that are right in some situations become wrong in others (i.e., when done for a bad end) but also those that are sometimes wrong become right when justified by a good

---

60. Ibid., p. 122.

61. Ibid., p. 124.

62. Cf. Paul Ramsey's energetic criticism of Fletcher's use of this passage; Ramsey, *Deeds and Rules in Christian Ethics*, p. 182.

63. Fletcher, *Situation Ethics*, p. 129.

end.[64] It is doubtful whether Fletcher can obtain support for this position from Paul. The statements in I Corinthians may be saying that things ordinarily good can become evil under certain circumstances. It is harder to read him as saying that something ordinarily evil becomes good if a good end is involved. But then, as Fletcher admits, Paul was victimized by the intrinsic theory.[65]

One of the objections that Fletcher anticipates and to which he responds is what he terms the "wedge" principle. Perhaps no harm would come if one person did this, but what would happen if *everybody did it?* This he believes to be a disguised form of Kant's abstract rule that an act to be moral must be *universally willed.* In this analysis, he would seem to be correct, albeit somewhat overly simplified.[66] He gives three replies.

He first says that there is no human act that would not lead to evil under certain circumstances. Whereas the usual form of the statement is that the generalization is to be made only for exactly similar circumstances, he says that this is fleeing from the variety of life.[67] But this statement puts Fletcher in a dilemma. If he maintains it consistently, what is there to prevent this from falling into antinomianism? On the other hand, if he allows for some commonality of situations (not necessarily absolute identity), does he not become vulnerable to the generalization argument? Apparently, Fletcher has not really come to grips with the issue of how much similarity there is among situations and how much similarity makes two situations morally identical.

The second tactic of reply is to note that abuse does not bar use. For example, he says, take the argument against the use of contraceptives on the basis that if everyone used them people will stop having children. Actually, the argument is

---

64. Ibid., p. 130.

65. Ibid., p. 123.

66. Ibid., p. 130.

67. Ibid., pp. 130-131.

only germane to the issue of such exclusive use of contraceptives that no children are ever born to a given couple, not to the question whether they should ever be used at all by a couple.[68]

The final rebuttal is simply to psychoanalyze the objectors, a method he frequently employs. He says:

> The "generalization argument" . . . is actually one of the maneuvers used to discredit personal responsibility and leave law in control. It is a fundamentally anti-situational gambit. It is form of obstructionism, a delaying action of static morality.[69]

Fletcher makes one other observation, the implications of which are not fully clear. He enumerates four factors that must be considered in every situation, all of which are balanced on love's scales. These are:

1. The end
2. The means
3. The motive
4. The consequences (results in addition to the end intended)

He notes that legalism had often taken the position that to be wrong an action had only to be at fault on one of these counts, whereas to be right it had to be right on all four. His own position becomes a bit unclear, but he says that an action "is imperative *only if* the situation demands it for love's sake."[70]

DECISION-MAKING AS SITUATIONAL

There is finally a contrast between two types of moral decision-making: the prescriptive, or anticipatory, and the situational.

---

68. Ibid., p. 131.

69. Ibid., p. 131.

70. Ibid., pp. 128-129.

Fletcher believes there is a strong yearning in many human hearts for a prefabricated morality. This is an approach in which an attempt is made to anticipate as closely as possible just what the situation will be and then to determine the proper course of action. It is a matter of having certain rules or laws that are always valid, and simply determining or recognizing which of these applies at a given time.[71]

This desire for a prefabricated morality is a sign of moral and spiritual insecurity, according to Fletcher. In fact, he says, "People like to wallow or cower in the security of the law."[72]

By contrast, the situationist holds that no such prior determination can be made. One must accept his freedom and be willing to recognize that he cannot always correctly anticipate situations with any degree of precision. He must recognize that many decisions fall within the "ethical penumbra"—where matters are neither obviously black nor clearly white.[73]

That one cannot prepare his decisions in prefabricated fashion is illustrated by two instances that Fletcher cites. One deals with a shipwreck in which a lifeboat was filled with forty persons, twice its proper capacity. The first mate, in command of the boat, ordered most of the men into the sea. When they refused, Holmes, a seaman, pitched them out. The others were eventually rescued and the court found Holmes guilty of murder but recommended mercy. Fletcher, however, says that Holmes did a good thing. This was a *kairos*, a moment of decision, and the end justified the means.[74]

The other instance in many ways was opposite. When Captain Scott's expedition to the South Pole ran into trouble and was returning to the coast with no time to spare, one of

---

71. Ibid., p. 134.

72. Ibid.

73. Ibid., p. 135.

74. Ibid., p. 136.

the men was injured and had to be carried. Carrying the stretcher would slow them dangerously. It was another *kairos.* What should Scott do? Should he abandon the man to help assure that the rest would survive, or should he attempt to preserve him at the risk of the others' lives? The justice dimension would almost seem to dictate the former. Scott chose the latter and all perished. Here, however, Fletcher seems to approve of Scott's decision as much as he does Holmes's.[75]

The point is simply that one cannot formulate a set of principles in such a way that he could say, "Whenever the lives of a large number of persons are endangered, it is better to take the lives of one or a few, rather than risk the loss of many." This would be to return to the old, unbending legalism. One cannot set up situations in advance. There are no universally valid rules except to love. One can only decide when he is in the concrete situation.

There are several objections that Fletcher seems to be raising to prescriptive ethics:

1. It simply isn't being consistently practiced. It isn't practical. Many people pay lip service to moral laws, then constantly flout them in practice.[76]

2. The other escape from the dilemma is to try to conform reality to the rules. This results in a gross oversimplification of reality, however. There has to be an ignoring of specific details and a fitting of all of reality onto a sort of Procrustean bed.[77]

3. Fletcher maintains that Jesus was opposed to such ethical activity. He was constantly in conflict with the legalism of the Pharisees. One of the areas in which an attempt is often made to set up inviolable principles in advance is sex. Fletcher believes that the only teaching on the

---

75. Ibid.

76. Ibid., p. 137.

77. Ibid., p. 138.

subject of sex that one can find in Jesus' words is on adultery and an absolute condemnation of divorce, which is a correlative matter. Beyond that, He said nothing.

> He said nothing about birth control, large or small families, childlessness, homosexuality, masturbation, fornication or pre-marital intercourse, sterilization, artificial insemination, abortion, sex play, petting, and courtship. Whether any form of sex (hetero, homo, or auto) is good or evil depends on whether love is fully served.[78]

Similarly, Robinson says that Jesus' statements on sex dealt only with adultery or prostitutes. The word *porneia* always has association in the New Testament (as its derivation implies) with promiscuity, if not indeed prostitution.[79]

4. A sort of summary statement is that the prescriptive approach falsifies life. It fails to face "paradoxical ambiguities." The issues of life are not clear-cut. One cannot prepare a manual of behavior in advance of the situation without either grossly oversimplifying the situations or else making the code so complex and involved as to be completely impractical.[80]

What he is saying is that ethical judgments cannot be made in the abstract. The question "Is adultery wrong?" cannot be answered in that form. Fletcher would say, "I don't know. That all depends." He must be given a real situation, in all of its particularity.[81] Yet, inherent in his position seems to be the idea that one only has this situation, in all its particularity, when he is actually present within it. A hypothetical situation is really not a situation, he seems to say.

---

78. Ibid., p. 139.

79. Robinson, *Christian Morals Today*, p. 32.

80. Fletcher, *Situation Ethics*, p. 140.

81. Ibid., p. 143.

There are seven questions that the Christian situationist must ask in any situation: what? why? who? when? where? which? and how? The first three are answered for him by his faith. They are his universals. The *what* is love. The *why* is for God's sake. The *who* is his neighbors. But the other four can only be answered in the situation. They are, as he says, the *kairos* factors.[82]

---

82. Ibid., p. 142.

Relativism Applied: Problem Issues

The publications of Fletcher and Robinson produced a quick and powerful reaction. Many persons welcomed the position, finding in them what they regarded as a more cogent approach to ethical decision-making than they had experienced in legalism. Others reacted negatively in sermons, speeches, articles, reviews, and books. A number of these were collected into two separate volumes: *The Situation Ethics Debate*[1] and *Storm Over Ethics.*[2] Interest was high, and "situation ethics" was a household expression in many church circles. Since about 1969, however, the furor seems to have quieted somewhat. Thus, Charles Curran could write in 1970: "The fascination with the situation ethics debate has waned in the last two years."[3] This is not to say that the debate has died completely. Such publications as John Macquarrie's *Three Issues in Ethics*[4] and Joseph Fletcher

---

1. Harvey Cox, ed., *The Situation Ethics Debate* (Philadelphia: Westminster Press, 1968).

2. John C. Bennett, et. al., *Storm Over Ethics* (Philadelphia: United Church Press, 1967).

3. Charles E. Curran, *Contemporary Problems in Moral Theology* (Notre Dame, Ind.: Fides Publishers, 1970), p. 254.

4. John Macquarrie, *Three Issues in Ethics* (New York: Harper & Row, 1970).

and Thomas Wassmer's *Hello Lovers!*[5] are evidence that this approach to ethical decision-making is still very much alive, as are the reactions to it. Some of the thrusts of situation ethics not only have not declined in popularity and influence, they have continued to grow and spread. Thus the question must still be raised regarding the validity of these particular aspects of situationism. Even during the height of the furor provoked by standard situation ethics there was some consensus both by its proponents and their critics as to the crucial questions raised by this ethic, to which it had not given a clear or satisfactory answer. It is the pursuit of these questions that has contributed to the later developments beyond the classic controversy.

Perhaps the key element in situationism is a shift away from an emphasis upon law or rules in formulating a moral decision. This is a matter of degree, since even the most determined legalist scarcely failed to recognize the central place of love in the Christian ethic, and hardly any situationist could be justly accused of totally disregarding laws or rules or principles. It is the proportionate influence of the two types of considerations that has undergone alteration.

Much of the later discussion has centered about the meaning of love. If a course of action is justified not by appeal to a rule or set of rules but simply on the basis that it is the most loving thing to do, just what constitutes "loving"? What does love strive to bring about in the life of the one who is loved?

Not all love ethics are situation ethics, despite the situationists' loud acclaim of love. Further, not all situationists have given or would give the same response to the challenges implicit in the question of the preceding paragraph. One rather widespread reply, however, was inherent in Fletcher's original statement of presuppositions. Here, the good is identified with what works, that is, with helpful

---

5. Joseph Fletcher and Thomas Wassmer, *Hello Lovers: An Invitation to Christian Ethics*, ed. William E. May (New York: World Publishing Co., 1970).

consequences. This, however, pushes the discussion a bit further by posing yet another question: What does it mean "to work" or "to help"? To put it differently: if the test of an action is the consequences that flow from it, how are those consequences to be evaluated?[6]

Before proceeding, it is important to pause briefly to note the growing pervasiveness of this emphasis. On the one hand, and rather evidently, those who have placed the prime emphasis upon consequences have done so in one of two ways. Some have virtually disregarded principles and have judged the act solely by its consequences. Others, however, have attempted to retain principles or even rules but have suggested that they must be abandoned or supplanted or set aside under certain conditions. These conditions are present when retaining the principles would lead to less desirable consequences than abandoning them.

A more subtle variety of consequentialism is found among those who ostensibly desire to retain the principles or rules and govern their actions by them. In the process of justifying a law-ethic some of these attempt to do so by appealing to experiential consequences. Some of the notable efforts to confirm the rightness of an absolute prohibition of premarital sex rely heavily upon empirical evidence, purporting to show the adverse effects of such premarital sex upon psychological health and even physical health. Although it is the principle of the law that justifies the action, there is a tendency to justify the principle by appeal to the consequences. It does raise the question of what would be the ultimate justification of an action, should principle and consequences conflict.

The consequentialist answer does lead to further questions: what will be the consequences of my action, and how will I determine what these consequences will be? If I know the consequences, how do I evaluate them? Part of the problem is the delimiting of a consequence. If I act, there will be an immediate consequence that will lead to another

---

6.   John G. Milhaven, "Objective Moral Evaluation of Consequences," *Theological Studies* 32, no. 3 (September 1971): 410.

consequence, which in turn will give birth to yet another consequence. Or an action may have consequences leading in two or more different directions.

One increasingly common means of answering these questions is through appeal to experience of a scientific nature. Here, either by clinical observation or by experimentation in physical and behavioral sciences, conclusions are drawn as to "good" and "helpful" actions. Numerous examples of this approach could be cited, and in the following pages this type of reasoning will be traced in several specific areas of morality. This introduces a certain type of objectivity and precision not often found in ethical discussions. Such a method draws ethical statements from empirical data without appearing to use a specifically ethical methodology.[7]

Two lines of reasoning seem to be followed in this scientific research. One is to determine what is indeed the case and thus is, in one sense of the word, "normative." Polls showing trends in attitude and practice are of this type. Who will forget the famous Kinsey reports? These purported to show that certain types of behavior commonly believed to be widely disapproved in society and practiced by only a small minority were actually rather widespread. If indeed such large numbers of persons engaged in the seemingly forbidden behavior, can the consequences really be as dire as has been thought? So seemed to be the reasoning. More direct, however, are the scientific examinations of the effects of certain types of behavior apart from the question of its prevalence. Much of the discussion of drug abuse has drawn upon this type of research, and the arguments for and against legalization of marijuana have to a large extent resulted from dependence upon conflicting sets of research data.

What has occurred is a shift from any type of deductive approach to an almost exclusively inductive method. In the

---

7. Ibid., pp. 410-412; cf. Eugene B. Borowitz, *Choosing a Sex Ethic: A Jewish Inquiry* (New York: Schocken Books, 1970), p. 123, and James Gustafson, "Responsibility and Utilitarianism" *Commonweal* 91, no. 5 (October 1969): 141.

deductive method certain principles, rules, or laws were believed to be binding. The major problem then was to determine whether the moral issue in question fell under one of these laws. The inductive way, on the other hand, was to derive principles from the data under examination. These principles are regarded as tentative, incomplete, and only probable. There is, in effect, a bypassing of any idea of special revelation. Revelation, if it enters into consideration at all, is more of the nature of general revelation.

It should be observed that Fletcher's emphasis upon love as the sole absolute seems to have faded somewhat in more recent developments. In Fletcher's ethic, there is a positive responsibility and impulse to love, to do constructive good. Today, however, there is more of an emphasis that whatever does not harm anyone else is good and permissible. Responsibility to others becomes largely a negative matter of not harming them; the positive responsibility is primarily to oneself.

PREMARITAL AND EXTRAMARITAL SEX

One of the areas that has received heaviest attention in recent ethical discussion involves sexual behavior. This is perhaps unfortunate since it helps reinforce the tendency to equate morality with sex. This is reflected in the legal terminology in which a "morals charge" is a sex offense. Robinson claims that the legalists' unbreakable laws are always related to sex, not war; yet he and Fletcher draw many of their most spectacular illustrations from the realm of sex.[8] Thus, to be selective and illustrative, the topics considered here will be drawn from several subdivisions of the general area of sex, where such an abundance of material is to be found.

For Fletcher, there are of course no invariable rules or absolute values other than love. Premarital or extramarital sex are right and good if they are the most loving thing to do,

8. John A. T. Robinson, *Christian Morals Today* (Philadelphia: Westminster Press, 1964), p. 17.

wrong if they are not. A young couple might decide to have premarital intercourse. This would be right if it were a responsible decision motivated by *agape*. It would not be right if it were a case of one member of the couple (it is assumed that it would be the boy) pressuring or manipulating the other into the act. He even suggests that a couple might decide to get the girl pregnant to obtain permission to marry from parents who were opposed, and that this would be right if done lovingly.[9]

Some later developments, however, seem to make less of the positive prescription of love. Here the emphasis falls more upon what is approved and accepted by society and upon the consequences of the action. In this latter respect, evidence from research in medical and behavioral sciences becomes particularly influential.

One example of a new shift going beyond the situationism of Fletcher and Robinson is found within the United Presbyterian Church U.S.A. The General Assembly of the Church on May 25, 1970 received a report on "Sexuality and the Human Community," prepared by a subcommittee of the Council on Church and Society. It represented two and one-half years of discussion by the committee and had been approved for presentation to the General Assembly by the parent council by a vote of 25 to 8.[10] The General Assembly voted 485 for and 259 against the document. The vote was not an adoption of this as a position paper, but rather was a recommendation of the materials to the churches for study.[11] Because of the size and significance of the United Presbyterian Church U.S.A., this must be regarded as a potent alternative in Christian ethics. As expected, the report has produced considerable controversy in the churches.

------

9. Joseph Fletcher, *Situation Ethics* (Philadelphia: Westminster Press, 1966), p. 104.

10. Jack Star, "The Presbyterian Debate Over Sex," *Look*, 11 August 1970, p. 54.

11. "United Presbyterians: Dropping the Traditional," *Christianity Today* 14, no. 19 (June 1970): 31.

The official Presbyterian policy on sex opposes "adultery, prostitution, fornication, and/or the practice of homosexuality." The new report is critical of these prohibitions, saying that whereas they may be necessary, the standing policy does not mention the Christian responsibility to glorify God by "the joyful celebration of delight in our sexuality." [12]

The report advocates a freer and more flexible policy on premarital sex than did the official position. It notes that a changed situation prevails from that which was extant when the older policy was adopted, and the stand of the church should take this into account. One dimension of this is the longer period that now exists between the onset of puberty and the culmination of marriage. Formerly, premarital virginity was expected to be preserved for a relatively short period of two to five years. Now this period may be extended to ten years or even more. This requires greater self-control and discipline.[13]

A second factor affecting the standards is the availability of easy and cheap contraception. Virginity was the main protection against the danger and fear of out-of-wedlock pregnancy. With the removal or at least diminution of this danger, virginity is less important.[14]

Further, young people's attitudes toward virginity have changed. Formerly, loss of virginity by a young woman was regarded as quite serious. Her "value" on the marital "market" was reduced, and she might actually be regarded as a fallen woman. To increasing numbers of young people, virginity per se means relatively little. More important is the general maturity of the person and readiness for marriage. A series of many intense but short-lived relationships, even

---

12. Star, "Presbyterian Debate Over Sex," p. 54.

13. Ibid., p. 60.

14. Ibid.

retaining technical virginity, would be regarded as more serious than mere loss of virginity.[15]

To summarize: the report suggests that nonvirginity may not be detrimental or harmful and that virginity may. Three reasons are offered: (1) virginity is now more difficult to maintain than formerly because of the lengthened period between puberty and marriage; (2) the danger of pregnancy is reduced; and (3) unfavorable social attitudes toward nonvirginity have diminished. Paired with these negative considerations are certain values that may attach to premarital intercourse.

Courtship should have the value of preparing for marriage. This should include developing "profound sensitivities to each other" and "tenderness in response to each other's needs and desires." This may include the decision to engage in premarital intercourse. The report says that if this decision has been made responsibly, the church "should not convey to them the impression that their decision is in conflict with their status as members of the body of Christ."[16] This might be interpreted as simply a reassurance that the church will not exclude such persons from its membership. This would not represent any real departure from past policy of the church, although some indication of repentance was often expected. Rather, the use of the expression "body of Christ" seems to suggest the view that premarital intercourse is not a sin for a Christian if it is under the conditions described here. This would then say that premarital intercourse not only is not wrong and sinful but under certain conditions could actually be good, as helping to prepare for successful marital adjustment. Here the case is not so much in terms of love but rather of the favorable

---

15. Ibid.; cf. three articles in *Church and Society* 60, no. 4 (March-April 1970): Herbert W. Richardson, "Evolution of Virginity," pp. 5-18; Margaret E. Kuhn, "Female and Single—What Then?" pp. 19-27; Richard P. Unsworth, "Today's Expectations of Premarital and Marital Sexual Behavior," pp. 28-35.

16. Star, "Presbyterian Debate Over Sex," p. 54.

consequences of the act. Left undiscussed at this point is the question of what happens when this period of premarital adjustment does not prove satisfactory to the partners involved.

The discussion is carried to this further issue later, however. Broader than simply preparing for marital adjustment is the value of sexual expression in developing a caring relationship. This must be recognized as an important aspect of human existence, and to deny it is to deny a natural part of man. Thus, with a growing number of single people, this cannot be restricted to the married and those about to be married. The statement says, "We question whether society has the right to impose celibacy or celibate standards on those who do not choose them." Here is a progression beyond the earlier statement. Now sexual expression (the use of the term "celibacy" suggests that sexual intercourse is included here) is not merely a preparation for marriage, it is in one of its effects an important aspect of human existence. Presumably, therefore, the church is wrong and is harming man in prohibiting premarital intercourse.[17]

The report also deals with the possiblity of communal living arrangements, both celibate and noncelibate. It suggests that the church at least has the obligation to explore such arrangements as "ethically acceptable and personally fulfilling alternatives of unmarried persons." The increased ratio of women to men in our society, particularly among older persons, calls for such exploration.[18]

There is also a suggestion that the church is lagging farther and farther behind "new developments" in modern life. Thus a generation is growing up that pays slight attention to what the church may have said on this and other issues in the past. Rather, these young people are looking elsewhere for their understanding of what constitutes a mature and healthy perspective on sex. The suggestion is that standards of sexual behavior are not determined by reference

17. Ibid.

18. Ibid.

to fixed rules but rather to what is mature and healthy, and that such judgments are derived from sources of information other than the church. Also implicit in this is the hint that the church is in danger of losing the younger generation because of its retention of outmoded (and unscientific?) views of sex.[19]

This position is well summarized in the report of one of the authors, the Reverend Richard P. Unsworth, chaplain and professor of religion at Smith College:

> Unfortunately, it's true that Christianity *has* been responsible for terrible sexual hang-ups. The church just hasn't been in touch with the realities of sexual behavior. It's incredible what's happened in the last 50 years and how greatly the significance of being a sexual human being has changed: the breakdown of large families to small family units; changes in contraceptive techniques (from coitus interruptus to the pill); the extension of single adult life, with girls maturing sexually at 12 and not marrying until their 20's.[20]

Not surprising, in view of these positions taken, is the committee's report on contraceptives. They recommend that contraceptives be given to any person desiring them. The extent of the recommendation is made clear by the following: "We consciously include, in the above recommendation, the availability of contraceptives to unmarried persons." This seemingly would imply at least tacit condoning of premarital sexual intercourse. The justification is the recognition of "changing folkways of nonmarital sexual conduct" in society. Many single persons are establishing sexual relationships, some of which anticipate marrige and some of which do not. Objection has sometimes been raised against disseminating contraceptives to single persons on the basis that it would encourage earlier and more intensive sexual exploration by young people, or would heighten the incidence of

---

19. Ibid.

20. Ibid.

promiscuity. The report, however, says of this suggestion that "the case is unproven."[21]

The one case in which objection is raised to the possibility of premarital intercourse by single young people reveals quite clearly the basis of the judgment. In a statement on dating, the committee notes the tendency of parents to push their young people into early dating out of fear that they might not be popular. The report expresses concern regarding this because some of these dating patterns lead to early experiences of sexual intercourse "badly out of phase with developing emotional maturity." The consequences can be quite harmful: undesirable psychological effects, an increased incidence of venereal disease, and out-of-wedlock pregnancy.[22] The implication is that this early dating should be discouraged and *for these reasons.*

More moderate is a statement adopted by the Lutheran Church in America in 1970. It was the result of four years' work of a ten-member committee appointed by the Board of Social Ministries. When the statement was presented to the biennial convention in Minneapolis in 1970, sharp debate was provoked. Among those delegates speaking critically of the statement was the governor of Minnesota, Harold LeVander, who commented, "We are saying that the laws of fornication are going to be wiped off the books. . . . We are proposing to reestablish common-law marriages." [23]

Perhaps the key expression in the entire document was "covenant of fidelity." This is the determinative factor in the discussion of marriage and is defined as "a dynamic, lifelong commitment of one man and one woman in a personal and sexual union."[24] Although recognizing the need of the

---

21. Ibid., p. 59.

22. Ibid.

23. "Lutheran Sex Code: Covenant Above Contract," *Christianity Today* 14, no. 22 (July 1970): 32.

24. "Lutherans in America: Drawing Together or Pulling Apart?" *Christianity Today* 14, no. 21 (July 1970): 34.

sanction of civil law or marriage, the report notes that it is not a sufficient test of the relationship. There are marriages that have proper legal and civil status but do not really include this covenant of fidelity. On the other hand, there may be relationships that include a covenant of fidelity even though no legal contract exists.

As suggested in the quotation from Governor LeVander, the debate focused on whether this statement does or does not condone sexual intercourse outside of marriage. The statement was amended by the delegates to read:

> Because the Lutheran Church in America holds that sexual intercourse outside the marriage union is morally wrong, nothing in this statement . . . is to be interpreted as meaning that this church either condones or approves premarital and extramarital sexual intercourse. [25]

The somewhat ambiguous expression, "covenant of fidelity," was elucidated by amendment: "The existence of a true covenant of fidelity outside marriage as a legal contract is extremely hard to identify." Nonetheless, drafters of the document said that it could be interpreted as permitting sexual intercourse outside legal marriage for two persons intending a lifelong commitment to each other.

The Lutheran document is not quite so broad and permissive as the Presbyterian. By emphasizing the covenant of fidelity and implying that this is a lifelong commitment, the Lutherans have restricted this to those who are married, about to be married, or involved in a "marriage without a license," or a common-law marriage. After lengthy debate the twenty-two-hundred-word statement was approved with the amendments mentioned above. [26]

Closely allied to the question of premarital sex is extramarital sex. Both of the statements treated this less

---

25. "Lutheran Sex Code," pp.32-33.

26. Ibid., p. 32.

completely than premarital sex. It is mentioned, however, both directly and by implication, in both statements. Even Fletcher gave relatively light treatment to this area of sexual ethics (the famous case of Mrs. Bergmeier notwithstanding). He had spoken approvingly of the Wolfenden report, which indicated that no sexual act between two persons competent to give mutual consent should be prohibited, except when it involves seduction of minors or an offense against the public order.[27] Unfortunately, "offense against the public order" remains rather vague, and it is difficult to ascertain just what is meant by this. As everywhere else, of course, here also the principle of "the most loving thing" is the supreme criterion.

The Presbyterian statement generally advocates sexual fidelity. The report, however, indicates that there are exceptional circumstances where extramarital sexual activity "may not be contrary to the interests of a faithful concern for the well-being of the marriage partner." Such cases might include situations where one partner suffers permanent mental or physical incapacity. Such a judgment would, however, have to be made by and on the responsibility of the person who takes the exception.[28]

The Lutheran statement appears to be a bit more explicit on the subject. Dr. Paul M. Orso, a member of the LCA Board of Social Ministry, which commissioned the document, said that the basic stance of the statement would allow a sexual relationship between a married person and someone other than his spouse so long as a covenant of fidelity existed between the two partners. This would be regarded as proper even though a legal marriage contract with a husband or wife were still binding. This might be the case, for example, where personal or legal reasons prevented a divorce and where the covenant of fidelity had deteriorated in the legal marriage. This is in keeping with what seems to be the key assumption of the Lutheran statement: it is a

---

27. Joseph Fletcher, *Moral Responsibility* (Philadelphia: Westminster Press, 1967), pp. 99ff.

28. Star, "Presbyterian Debate Over Sex," p. 60.

covenant of fidelity, not a legal procedure, that really determines marriage. Where this exists, there is a marriage, whether a legal marriage has been enacted or not. Where it no longer exists, there is really no longer a marriage, even if no divorce decree has been granted.[29]

HOMOSEXUALITY

Increasing controversy has in recent years swirled about the subject of homosexuality. Although it does not appear that the number of homosexuals has particularly increased, they have become more visible. A sense of corporate identity seems to have developed among homosexuals. Gay communities have emerged, and even a gay church has been formed. At the University of Minnesota in 1971, an avowed homosexual was elected president of the student body, and his roommate, or "lover," who was denied a position on the university library staff, filed suit against the university on the ground that he had been discriminated against because he was a homophile. The two also made headlines when they attempted to be married. Like many other minorities, the homosexuals have become more aggressive, and the resulting publicity has helped to arouse and crystallize public opinion.

Here, as with premarital sex, we may detect the same shift from ethical principles to consideration of consequences. There appear to be two dimensions: a conclusion that the Bible, properly understood, either does not condemn homosexuality or is not applicable; and an observation that homosexuality is not "contrary to nature." One of the more thorough studies done on the subject was a consultation on "Theology and the Homosexual" sponsored by the Glide Urban Center and the Council on Religion and the Homosexual, held in San Francisco, August 22-24, 1966. As a sample of the trends of development, we might consult a paper by the Reverend Dr. Robert L. Treese on "Homo-

---

29. "Lutheran Sex Code," pp. 33.

sexuality: A Contemporary View of the Biblical Perspective."[30]

Treese begins by examining the biblical perspective on homosexuality. Although recognizing the abuse of the Bible by many, he indicates that it is still normative in the life of the church. His own view of the Bible is that it is not the Word of God. It is the words of men in and through which the "living, active, constantly contemporary Word of God" comes. A Bible passage is to be interpreted in terms of the experiences, life setting, and problems of its author as well as his purposes for writing. It is to be interpreted and explained in the light of our contemporary experience and knowledge. Whereas the Bible writers faced the same basic existential questions we do, their answers, like ours, are time-caught and thus valid only for them. The values affirmed by their answers are of significance for us. Finally, the whole Bible is to be seen in light of the gospel of Jesus Christ and the experience of the early church.[31]

Against this background Treese examines the relevant biblical passages. Five of these that seem to refer to homosexuality are seen to be King James mistranslations. In I Kings 14:22-24; 15:12; 22:46; II Kings 23:7; and Deuteronomy 23:17-18, there are references to what he believes to be a fertility cult flourishing in the temple at Jerusalem. The feminine noun *Qᵉdeshāh* was translated as "temple servant" (female) or "prostitute." The masculine form *(Qādhēsh, Qᵉdhēshim)* was rendered as "sodomite," the translators apparently thinking that it referred to a male homosexual temple prostitute. Treese, however, suggests that the idea of homosexual prostitutes serving in a fertility cult is utterly

---

30. Robert L. Treese, "Homosexuality: A Contemporary View of the Biblical Perspective" (Paper prepared for the Consultation on Theology and the Homosexual, sponsored by the Glide Urban Center and the Council on Religion and the Homosexual in San Francisco, August 22-24, 1966).

31. Ibid., p. 6.

incongruous. Thus, he proposes that the correct translation should be "male cult prostitute."[32]

A second area of biblical data concerns the cities of Sodom and Gomorrah and the destruction thereof. The traditional interpretation has been that the sin of these two cities was homosexuality and that it was anger against this sin that motivated Jehovah to destroy them. So prevalent has this view been that "sodomy" has come to be a synonym for homosexuality. Treese believes this is an incorrect understanding. When the two male angels came to the house of Lot, the men of the city came to Lot's house and demanded that he bring out the two visitors "that we may know them." When Lot offered them his two daughters instead, they became angry, and it was necessary for the angels to strike them with blindness. The next morning after Lot and his family had fled, the city was destroyed. Although the Hebrew word used here *yādha* (to know), was used 10 times in the Old Testament to denote sexual intercourse, this is only 10 such usages out of a total of 943 occurences in the Old Testament. It could well be translated here as "get acquainted with." He further argues that the interpretation that the sin of these cities was homosexuality did not really arise until the second century B.C. in nonbiblical writings of the Jews. It should be noted, however, that if many interpreters have misunderstood the intention of those men of Sodom, so apparently did Lot, in view of his offer of his daughters to them. In any event, Treese does not believe that the Sodom incident can be used as a biblical condemnation of homosexuality.[33]

There are six remaining specific biblical passages that must be grappled with. Two of these, Leviticus 18:22 and Leviticus 20:13, are found in the midst of passages proscribing certain grievous sins such as incest, intercourse during menstruation, and bestiality. He observes that these homosexual acts are mentioned in a listing of offenses attributed to

---

32. Ibid., pp. 7-8.

33. Ibid., pp. 8-12.

Egypt and Canaan. He therefore maintains that these homosexual acts are proscribed as an indication of idolatry, the reversal of the true order. His other observation is that the Jewish legal code has been superseded by the gospel of Jesus Christ. Ignoring any distinction between moral and ceremonial law, he suggests that it is inconsistent to accept Leviticus 20:13 and to reject, for example, Leviticus 20:25 ("You shall therefore make a distinction between the clean beast and the unclean").[34]

This principle, if accepted, would seem to rule out effectively any Old Testament reference. A similar stance is taken in a leaflet, "Homosexuality, What the Bible Does . . . And Does Not Say!" written by Miss Kim Stablinski and distributed by Metropolitan Community Church of Los Angeles, a congregation of homophiles: She says:

> What does the Bible actually say about homosexuality? Let's not check the Old Testament references, for in with the few comments on the subject there we will be distracted by such sins as eating rabbit (Leviticus 11:6), lobster, clams, shrimp, oysters (Leviticus 17:10)—or of wearing garments "of divers sort, as of woolen and linen together" (Deuteronomy 22:11, KJV).[35]

This leaves four New Testament references that purport to speak directly about the matter of homosexuality. These are Romans 1:26 and 27, I Corinthians 6:10, and I Timothy 1:10. By way of summary of his findings, Treese says of these that they

> indicate with no possibility of qualification that homosexual practices were considered by Paul (and the writer of I Timothy) as concrete sins on a par with adultery and murder, as evidence of the original sin with which the human race is infected. Thus the moral question has been illuminated somewhat, but the theological issue of

---

34. Ibid., pp. 12-14.

35. Kim Stablinski, "Homosexuality, What the Bible Does . . . And Does Not Say!" (Brochure distributed by the Metropolitan Community Church, Huntington Park, Calif.).

homosexuality remains unopened in the New Testament.[36]

Thus for Treese the examination of the biblical data is only preliminary. The context for theological discussion must be set from two perspectives: a consideration of the causality and definition of homosexuality, and meditation on the meaning of the writer's personal knowledge of homosexuals. For theological knowledge to be true to its essential nature, it must be grounded in contemporary phenomena and knowledge.[37] He defines the homosexual as one who has a "definite preferential erotic attraction to members of the same sex."[38] He notes that there is no single homosexual personality type and that apart from this one characteristic a homosexual may be as much like a heterosexual person as any two persons can be alike. The question of causation is a complex one, however, and the origins are seen now to be multifactorial, including sociocultural, psychodynamic, biological, and situational.

Of particular interest is Treese's investigation of the possibility that neither heterosexuality nor homosexuality is normal or natural in the human being. He notes evidence suggesting that at birth a human being is psychosexually neutral. This potential permits the human to develop in any of several diverse patterns. The basic biological drives are relatively "unfocused." The direction of these drives and the objects to which they become attached are determined by the experiences of learning and reinforcement that the individual receives from his environment. Thus there is nothing abnormal or unnatural about homosexuality. The "abnormality" is simply that our society generally condemns this type of behavior and consequently it leads to certain difficulties and handicaps for the person who engages in it. The psychiatrist's clinical evidence of abnormality in homo-

---

36. Treese, "Homosexuality: A Contemporary view." p. 17.

37. Ibid., p. 18.

38. Ibid., p. 19.

sexuals is scarcely determinative, since by the nature of the case those who seek psychiatric help would constitute a rather skewed sample. If the "normality" of heterosexuals were evaluated on the basis of psychiatrists' clinical data, the judgment might well emerge that heterosexuals as a group are abnormal. Thus, the theological construct whereby homosexuality is regarded as "abnormal" may well be socioculturally conditioned. The theologian must ask the hard question of the helpfulness of such a concept as well as of the effectiveness of a culturally accommodated church.[39]

This leads him to the second area of contemporary reflection: his personal experience with homosexuals. He observes that he has seen "gay" persons accept Christ and join His body. Evidently the grace of God was not withheld from them. Likening the situation of the church with respect to such persons to that of Peter in relationship to Cornelius, he raises the question whether homosexuality can be "right" for some persons. He tells of homosexuals whom he has come to know and admire who are mature and responsible persons. He recognizes the tremendous "hell" through which they have had to go because of the constant threat of ruination of their lives, loss of jobs and social standing, if their true natures were known to employers and the authorities. Despite this mental harassment by society they are committed to relationships that are fulfilling and have redemptive qualities. He does not apply to his evaluation of these persons any preset principles, whether biblically derived or otherwise. Rather, he says:

> The plumbline of judgment must be my own perception of the capacity of these persons for openness to other human beings, for mature and responsible social involvements and for love in its fulfilling depth. I must, in the face of the church's "no" speak a loud "yes" to these persons, for I have seen the marks of self-giving Christian love upon their lives.[40]

---

39. Ibid., pp. 21-23.

40. Ibid., pp. 24-25.

Treese disputes the tendency of much theology to equate ontologically the fact that God created man and woman with obvious physical sexual differentiation with the psychosexual expression of this sex differentiation. What it means to be a human being does not hinge on heterosexual relationships. Rather, the critical factor is a "I-Thou" relationship to another human being. He sees the possibility of mutual love, empathy, confidentiality, and trust within a homosexual union. Some homosexual couples whom he has known have developed highly successful relationships over periods of ten and even twenty-five years.[41]

Although it is true that such enduring relationships among homosexuals are rare, he argues that this can be fully accounted for by the tremendous pressures that the homosexual faces from society. The ostracism and the necessity of hypocrisy must be endured without the support of a legal relationship, informed by a traditional ethos, such as the institution of marriage. When allowance is made for all of this, and when comparison is made with the relative lack of permanence in heterosexual marriages, homosexual relationships do not appear in quite so unfavorable a light. The aim of the church is to help lead persons into significant self-affirming and other-affirming relationships. When allowance is made for the problems that may not be inherent in homosexual relationships, Treese says:

> It would seem that logically and theologically there is no reason to deny the possibility of marriage to the homosexual couple, subject to the same privileges and restrictions that inhere in heterosexual marriages.[42]

The Presbyterian statement, to which reference has already been made, shows both similarities to and differences from this position paper. It notes that Paul's condemnation of homosexualism occurs in a list of antisocial and personally destructive forms of conduct and is not singled out as worse

---

41. Ibid., p. 31.

42. Ibid., p. 32.

than these other "sins." The context of these condemnations suggests that Paul objected to the element of disregard for the neighbor, more than to acts in themselves. The homosexual and heterosexual are not on that basis and differently related to God. Neither is exempt from the experience of alienation from God and both therefore are eligible for the experience of reconciliation in Christ.[43]

The problem with homosexual behavior, according to the Presbyterian paper, is not that it is sinful but rather that it is essentially incomplete in character. Care should therefore be exercised to guard against the development of fixed homosexual patterns during childhood and adolescence. Education is especially important. Recognizing that homosexuality may well be fostered in "unisexual" institutions such as separate men's and women's schools, penal institutions, and the armed forces, the report recommends that the church endeavor to use its influence to change the nature of such institutions. Some steps toward such a rectification would include conjugal visitation rights for prisoners and furloughs in the community. Laws that make a felony of homosexual acts privately committed by consenting adults should be repealed. Note that in this statement the consideration is not whether any ethical principles are violated. Rather, the distinguishing factor is that homosexual behavior is incomplete in nature.[44] This does go beyond Treese's statement by suggesting that homosexuality may be undesirable and disadvantageous, and it appears to be saying that this undesirability is inherent in the act, rather than a result of societal pressures.

In the Lutheran statement, the original form as presented to the assembly classified homosexual activity as a "deviation" from the heterosexual structure of God's creation. The statement as adopted, however, substituted the word "departure" for "deviation." It further affirmed that persons who engage in homosexual activity are sinners only

---

43. Star "Presbyterian Debate Over Sex," p 59.

44. Ibid.

as are all other persons. Delegates made attempts on the convention floor to introduce amendments suggesting that homosexuals need to be cured through medical or spiritual help. These, however, were roundly defeated.[45]

There is a discernible trend in these several statements. On the one hand, although acknowledging the several rather clear and definite biblical statements opposing homosexuality, there is the suggestion that the Bible is not to be considered normative or binding for today. Rather, evaluation must be made on the basis of contemporary data. Here the conclusion seems to be that homosexuality may not really be abnormal, and that for some persons it may even be "right." It does not necessarily have inherent unfortunate consequences, any undesirable effects being largely a result of unwholesome attitudes and treatment by society. What is needed is a revision of society's attitudes rather than insistence upon attempted cure of the homosexual, although the Presbyterian statement urges effort to prevent children and young people from falling into permanent patterns of homosexuality because of its incompleteness.

ABORTION

Abortion has also been a topic of wide discussion. This has come to the fore as a result of legislative proposals in several states for a liberalization of existing abortion statutes. This has thrust the issue from the comparative oblivion of the ethics classroom into the brightly lighted arena of political debate with attendant publicity given by the press and the mass media. Simultaneous with this, and to some extent causing it, has been the women's rights movement with its insistence (at least in some segments of the movement) upon each woman's self-determination of whether and when she shall give birth.

Much traditional discussion of the topic has proceeded from theological and moral principles. The topic of when life really begins or when there is a person or a self (or in

---

45. "Lutheran Sex Code," p. 33.

theological terms, a "soul") has been energetically debated, with Roman Catholic moralists especially attempting to focus the discussion upon this point. This has been regarded as crucial since, if the fetus that is removed from the uterus is actually a human person, abortion would seem to be a species of murder.

Recent discussion in Christian ethics has tended to move away from this orientation to abortion. In part, this appears to result from the view that the question of the beginning of life cannot really be resolved and thus that a principled or deductive ethical methodology is impossible. A wide variety of views has been proposed: that the beginning of the human person is to be dated from conception (up to seventy-two hours after coitus), implantation (seven days), the final fixing of the genetic code (three weeks), the first central nervous system activity (eight weeks), brain development and cardiac activity (twelve weeks), quickening (sometime after the twelfth week), viability (between the twentieth and twenty-eighth weeks), and birth.[46] There has been no consensus regarding the proper fixing of the beginning of life (even as there is no universally accepted definition of the cessation of life). Even theologians have been unable to agree upon the relationship of the soul to the fetus.[47]

In the light of this, the shift has been away from an ethical view requiring an *undifferentiated* concern for life, toward an emphasis upon *personal* life and upon the *quality* of life.[48] Many persons today do not see in the embryo more

---

46. "Freedom of Choice Concerning Abortion," *Social Action* 38, no. 1 (September 1971): 10.

47. Articles in Walter O. Spitzer and Carlyle L. Saylor, eds., *Birth Control and the Christian.* (Wheaton, Ill.: Tyndale House, 1969): cf. Bruce K. Waltke, "Old Testament Texts Bearing on the Problem of the Control of Human Reproduction," pp. 7-23; Robert P. Meye, "New Testament Texts Bearing on the Problem of the Control of Human Reproduction," pp. 27-47; Paul K. Jewett, "The Relationship of the Soul to the Fetus," pp. 51-66.

48. "Freedom of Choice Concerning Abortion," p. 10.

than the *potentiality* of human personhood. Here again the primary consideration becomes the consequences of the two alternatives. The Eighth General Synod of the United Church of Christ in its discussion of abortion reform put it this way:

> The implication is that factors other than its [the embryo's] existence may appropriately be given equal or greater weight at this time—the welfare of the whole family, its economic condition, the age of the parents, their view of the optimum number of children consonant with their resources and the pressures of population, their vocational and social objectives, for example.[49]

Beyond the theoretician's activity was that of the practicing minister and counselor. One of the most emphatic statements of this position is found in an article, "Abortion: Woman's Right and Legal Problem," by Howard Moody. Moody is pastor of Judson Memorial Church in New York City and a Director of the New York Civil Liberties Union. He was a leader in the founding of the Clergy Consultation Service on Abortion. This organization referred thousands of women for safe abortions and supported passage of legislation legalizing abortion in New York. Such a bill, permitting abortions by licensed physicians within the first twenty-four weeks of pregnancy, was passed in 1970. Moody contrasts the theoretical approach that screamed "Murder!" whenever the subject of abortion liberalization was raised, with the actual involvement with pregnant women:

> But the actual process of working with women compelled us to move beyond strictly theoretical hang-ups. In this process we always had to consider the moral question of whether it is justifiable to force the unwanted upon the unwilling. In our anxiety to honor the theory of the sanctity of life in *general*, we have played fast and loose with *particular* women's lives and forced them by legal fiat to bear children that they never intended to conceive. To use a woman's body, *against her free will and choice*, as a receptacle for unwanted pregnancy has got to be seen as a kind of

---

49. Ibid.

"legalized rape" that must be as morally repugnant as "feticide" to those perpetrating it.[50]

Forcing a woman to give birth to an unwanted child is therefore the first reason for favoring the easier availability of abortion. The second is the "third party." He notes that with all the discussion of rights of the fetus, there is very little mention of the unwanted, unborn child's chances for a happy life. The unwanted and consequently frequently unloved child often has a malformed spirit and a mutilated psyche. Furthermore, he claims, the child abuse syndrome is directly related to resented and unloved children.[51]

A third consideration is the larger society in which we live and for which we are responsible. We live in a time in which the exploding population is a social problem of major proportions. It is becoming apparent that there simply are not adequate resources in our world to permit unchecked and unplanned reproduction of the race. It may be that we are approaching a situation where allowing a fetus to develop and be born will mean choosing that some living person must die. In view of this crushing problem of population explosion, talk about the right to be born seems a bit cavalier.[52]

From the foregoing, the pattern seems rather clearly to be the formulation of ethical conclusions and action, not out of theological reflection or upon moral principles but rather from the context of actual contact with the persons involved and empathetic response to their needs and predicaments.

The United Church of Christ's recommendation on abortion follows much the same contour. The statement indicates that the present rather restrictive laws are neither just nor enforceable. The two alternatives for a woman who has an unwanted pregnancy are equally undesirable: either bearing an unwanted child, with the unfortunate effects both

---

50. Howard Moody, "Abortion: Woman's Right and Legal Problem," *Theology Today* 28, no. 3 (October 1971): 338.

51. Ibid., p. 339.

52. Ibid.

for the mother and the child; or seeking an illegal abortion, regardless of the medical hazards and suffering that may result. Further, because of severely limiting access to safe abortions, the present laws of most states have the effect of discriminating against the poor. Well-to-do women can travel to Scandinavia for an abortion; the poor cannot.[53]

The action of the Eighth General Synod of the United Church of Christ therefore recommends the repeal of all legal prohibitions of physician-performed abortions. This would take abortion completely out of the realm of penal law and place the decision in the hands of the principals. Voluntary and medically safe abortions would be legally available to all women. Two other provisions were also included in the recommendation. One was that adequate protection should be given to "conscientious objectors" against abortion, including physicians, nurses, and prospective mothers. The other emphasized the importance of adequate counseling for the woman contemplating an abortion.[54]

The Presbyterian statement follows much the same pattern, advocating the removal of abortion from the legal realm entirely and making it a matter of the careful ethical decision of a woman, her physician, and her pastor or other counselor. It is cautious about blanket approval of ethical decisions to have an abortion. Counseling is vital in this matter. Specifically mentioned is the potential panic associated with many unwanted pregnancies. Possible alternative means of resolving problem pregnancies must be adequately explored. Similar consideration should be given to "the possible effects of a contemplated abortion on both parties to the conception and on other family members." While stressing the preferability of contraception, this statement insists that when for any reason contraception fails and an unwanted pregnancy results, it is not "compassionate or just to insist that available help be withheld."[55]

---

53. "Freedom of Choice Concerning Abortion," p. 11.

54. Ibid.

55. Star, "Presbyterian Debate Over Sex," pp. 59-60.

John Milhaven, in a helpful article on "The Abortion Debate: An Epistemological Interpretation," suggests that those favoring abortion tend to justify it on the basis of the experiential consequences of the persons involved. Since, however, unborn fetuses either do not have experiences or, if they do, are not able to report them, the decision is focused upon the experience of others: the mother, the immediate family, or even of society in general. It is the shift from a principle orientation (such as the inviolability of human life) to an experience orientation that has in effect determined the outcome of the decision.[56]

---

56. John G. Milhaven, "The Abortion Debate: An Epistemological Interpretation," *Theological Studies* 31, no. 1 (March 1970): 112-115.

Critique
of Relative Ethics

THE POSITIVE CONTRIBUTIONS OF
SITUATIONISM AND CONSEQUENTIALISM

There is value in any movement that arises as a protest against an excessive or distorted view. By pointing out the shortcomings of legalism and by emphasizing some of the neglected themes of Chritian ethics, the situationists and their heirs, the consequentialists, have done us a considerable favor. Whereas the major portion of this chapter will be devoted to pointing out what seem to this writer to be deficiencies of these ethical methods, he is appreciative of several helpful contributions that they have made to ethical discourse.

Recognition of the Difficulty of Moral Decision-Making

First, these men have pointed out the extreme difficulty and complexity involved in making moral decisions. There are several aspects to this. The first is determining precisely the nature of the values or principles by which one is to guide his moral action. The second problem is how to determine whether a given case is an instance of one of these values and, if so, which one. Another way of putting this is that the problem is determining what principle applies in a given situation. Further, there is the difficulty of knowing the relative place to assign to these various factors, or how to determine which neighbor to attend to first.

These determinations and decisions frequently are not arrived at easily. Often the difficulty in decision-making is not a choosing between the obviously good and the obviously bad. It is to distinguish the better from the good and the best from the better. Hence, Walter Judd, former U.S. Congressman from Minnesota, described the difficulties facing a legislator. A bill appears for consideration. The bill is in the judgment of the congressman basically a good bill, but it contains a rider which he judges to be a bad or immoral consideration. Said Dr. Judd, "The problem is this. Shall I vote 'yes' to enact the good bill and with it get the bad feature contained in the rider? Or shall I vote 'no' to kill the bad rider and lose the basic bill in the same process? That is the difficulty. Often I pray during the roll call, down through all the Johnsons, that when they call Judd I will know which way to vote."[1] It is not only congressmen who face dilemmas like this. These are part of the texture of life. Classical terminology spoke of "doing the lesser of two evils." Fletcher would prefer to describe it as finding the right and good thing to do. Either way, the problem in its several manifestations mentioned above is undeniably present in much of life.

Acknowledgement of Life's Diversity

One prime tenet, perhaps the central assertion of relativism, is that there are a variety of situations that occur, and that variations are to be found even among those quite similar. Consequently, no ethical system can work out detailed laws covering every situation, actual or possible. This observation proves true with respect to the Bible, for example. If the Bible were to prescribe a law to deal with every imaginable circumstance, no one could carry his Bible under his arm or in his pocket. To take one's Bible with him would require the use of a moving van. It simply does not contain that many explicit and detailed references.

---

1. Walter Judd, "Congressman Judd Talks to Young People About Politics," *United Evangelical Action* 20, no. 2 (April 1961): 9.

Emphasis upon Faultiness of Some Human Statutes

The situationists have underscored the very faulty or at least imperfect character of many human legal formulations. An example cited by Fletcher is a law in England requiring that a marriage to be recognized legally must be validated by physical consummation; this resulted in a child born by artificial insemination by the husband being declared illegitimate.[2] Every municipality has laws on the statute books that once were useful but that now have been outgrown. Some of these still are being enforced; others are not. There are other laws that always have been unjust or unwise. The civil rights movement of the past few years has focused upon some of these that are discriminatory.

When laws such as these are combined with an overly zealous spirit of adherence to the letter of the law, ludicrous situations may result. Hence, in what may be a sincere and conscientious effort, persons may be hurt and the law preserved. Note that the law, being impersonal, is not conscious of this and is not profited, so that no one wins.

It is true, also, that legalism can result in justifying the doing of a mere minimum. Whereas laws are generally intended to guarantee that at least a minimum will be done, they can be used to justify doing only that minimum. This is law perverted into legalism. This is not a necessary feature of a law—or principle—ethic. The law could be so ordered as to command a maximum. Indeed, it is this that has motivated some to describe as a new legalism situationism's dictum to practice *agape* always and everywhere.

Highlighting of Personal Values

This forms a natural transition to a fourth favorable point, namely, that situationism and consequentialism have rightly recalled us to personalism. The ethic of the Bible is not a cold listing of rules and codes that run roughshod over personal values. Jesus underscored this when He said, "The

---

2. Joseph Fletcher, *Situation Ethics* (Philadelphia: Westminster Press, 1966), pp. 78-79.

sabbath was made for man, and not man for the sabbath" (Mark 2:27). Note that He thereby gave some content to what the good for man is, namely rest, health, and worship. When what was intended to be the means to an end is elevated into an end in itself, you have a type of idolatry. In the Bible this is extended not only to concern for finite human persons, but also to pursuit of the honor and "welfare" of the Supreme Person, God. This latter dimension of Christian personalism is not always emphasized in the writings of Fletcher and Robinson.

Centering of Ethics on Love

Situation ethics agrees with the Bible in stressing love. Jesus, having stated the first two great commandments as loving God with all one's being—heart and mind and soul and strength, and loving one's neighbor as oneself, went on to indicate that the entire law "hung" upon these two points (Matthew 22:37-40). Fletcher has given an excellent delineation of love in his chapter "Loving Is Not Liking," which, in this writer's judgment, is by far the best chapter in *Situation Ethics*. He has correctly captured the essence of love as concern for the ultimate welfare of the other and action directed to that end, and not as merely sentimental feeling.

Motivation Made Decisive

Finally, situationism has emphasized the moral significance of the motive rather than merely the formal act. Jesus underscored this in the Sermon on the Mount when He indicated that not murdering one's fellowman did not necessarily constitute good. It is also a question of whether one is angry with his brother (Matthew 5:21-22). Purity is more than abstention from the physical act of adultery. As Jesus appraised it, lusting after a woman in one's heart was a case of adultery (Matthew 5:27-28). The inward attitude was of importance, in His judgment.

Beyond the formal fact of chastity one really must ask the reason. Is it because of fear of infection, detection, and pregnancy? Or is it because of a conviction that premarital and extramarital sexual intercourse is wrong, whether one experiences any inexpedient consequences or not? This is a good question, for it presses the consideration beyond "What do I do?" to "Why do I do it?" It is a point which situationism has again placed in a position of prominence.

FAULTS OF SITUATIONISM
AND CONSEQUENTIALISM

Problems of Instability

In introducing situationism, Fletcher relates it to two other approaches to decision-making. The first is legalism, in which solutions are preset and absolute. They have been worked out in advance, or are believed to have been revealed by God, and can therefore be "looked up" in a book and followed. There is also antinomianism, which does not bring into the decision-making situation any principles, maxim, or any rules whatsoever. It derives the ethical solution from the situation itself. In contrast to these, situationism comes to the situation of decision fully armed with the moral wisdom of the past, but prepared to drop or modify these maxims if, in a given situation, love would be better served by doing so.

William Frankena, drawing upon the work of John Rawls,[3] has devised a set of designations that seem to be helpful in analyzing the different approaches, considering each in relationship to love.[4] Rule-agapism affirms that there are certain rules or at least principles that when followed are productive of love. Legalism would be of this type. In act-agapism there are no rules, only acts, that count for love. Antinomianism seems to be an instance of this. Summary rule-agapism regards rules or principles as summaries of what

---

3. Joseph Rawls, "Two Concepts of Rules," *Philosophical Review* 64 (1955): 3-32.

4. William Frankena, "Love and Principle in Christian Ethics," *Faith and Philosophy*, ed. Alvin Plantinga (Grand Rapids: Eerdmans Publishing Co., 1964), pp. 203-225.

acts have in the past been loving, but not as fixed absolutes of love. These would be regarded as guides to what love might mean in the present and the future, but not as absolute or infallible guides. This is where situationism apparently is to be placed, since it regards its principles as summaries that are to be set aside if they are not love-serving.

The question that must now be asked concerns the stability and objectivity of the situational. Can situationism retain the mediating position of summary rule-agapism, or does it tend to slide either in the direction of pure rule-agapism (legalism) or act-agapism (antinomianism)?

It should be apparent initially that Fletcher's sharpest criticisms are directed at legalism. In most cases, these are criticisms with which the antinomian could also agree. Hence, it should be in order to ask first whether in practice his view is distinguishable from antinomianism. The difference should appear in the situationist's use of the maxims. Just how, then, do the maxims function in practice?

The Role of Maxims. In the cases that Fletcher cites, the situation seems always to be turned against the principles or maxims, requiring alterations or modifications in them. Thus, although the maxims are described as illuminators (but not directors) of the decision-making process, in practice they seemingly tend to impede correct judgment.[5]

To put it differently: just how do the maxims illuminate the moral decision-making process? Presumably, the maxims, as summaries of past moral wisdom, are to be followed unless there is basis to feel that this would not be the most loving course to follow. But what would be the criteria of whether the maxims are to be set aside? Unless some content is given to love, the situation itself becomes the basis for determining whether the maxim is to be followed. In this case, situa-

5. Paul Ramsey, *Deeds and Rules in Christian Ethics* (New York: Charles Scribner's Sons, 1967), pp. 147-148; Joseph Fletcher, "Love Is the Only Measure," *Commonweal* 83, no. 14 (January 1966): 428; John G. Milhaven, review in *Theological Studies* 27, no. 3 (September 1966): 484.

tionism would seem at most to differ only in degree from antinomianism of the type described by Fletcher. Whether such constituting and defining content is given to love must of course be determined.

Another way of formulating it is this: what counts for love? Are there really any circumstances or set of circumstances that would render a course of action loving? If love is what makes something good and "unlove," or indifference, makes it evil, is there anything that always counts for love or, at least, is always identified with love? Is there any way really to detect the presence of love and thereby to rule on the morality of a given course of action?

Arbitrariness of Decision. The problem may be crystallized by observing two cases that Fletcher juxtaposes. The first concerns an incident in 1841 in which the ship *William Brown* struck an iceberg and sank. In one of the two boats that got away there were forty persons, twice as many as the boat could safely hold. When the first mate ordered most of the males into the sea, they refused, and Holmes, a seaman, pitched them out of the boat. Although a court convicted Holmes of murder, but with mercy recommended, Fletcher says that his action was a good thing.[6]

The other action seems in some ways to be almost the opposite. During Captain Scott's expedition to the South Pole, one of his men was seriously injured and to carry him would dangerously slow the party. This Scott chose to do rather than abandoning the man, and consequently the entire party perished. Fletcher approves also of Scott's decision, provided it was not simply made legalistically.[7]

Here are two cases that seem similar. Indeed, in their essential features they appear virtually identical. In some ways, it would seem easier to approve of a decision by Scott to leave the injured man than Holmes' throwing out the men, since this latter involved a positive act that resulted in their

---

6. Fletcher, *Situation Ethics*, p. 136.

7. Ibid.

death, whereas the former only required omission of action—just leaving him there. Fletcher approves of both actions, although they are virtually contradictory. It may well be that there are specific points of difference between the two cases, which make putting the few to death to save the several the good thing to do in the one case, while risking (and losing) the lives of all in the attempt to save one man was good in the other. But Fletcher does not call attention to any such particular considerations. Rather, the impression he gives is that either course of action would have been good in either case, so long as the decision is not made on a legalistic basis.[8] If this is so, then it would seem that "good" is not a qualifying adjective attaching to a particular course of action and dependent upon what action is taken. Rather, it is a function of the way in which an action is done, irrespective of what action it is.

Vagueness of the Concept of Love. This suggests that situationism has greater affinity with antinomianism than was initially claimed. Anything is good if it is done lovingly. But what is involved in acting lovingly? Are there any actions incompatible with love? If not, just what is love? Is the definition of love purely connotative, or does it denote any actions at all?[9]

---

8. Ramsey, *Deeds and Rules*, pp. 216-217.

9. This problem has been pointed out by numerous commentators, among them: James M. Gustafson, "How Does Love Reign?" *Christian Century* 83, no. 18 (May 1966): 654; C. Peter Wagner, "Is Love Enough?" *Eternity* 18, no. 2 (February 1967): 59; John M. Swomley, Jr., review in *Fellowship* 33 (November 1966), reprinted in Harvey Cox, ed., *The Situation Ethics Debate* (Philadelphia: Westminster Press, 1968), p. 88; Henlee H. Barnette, *The New Theology and Morality* (Philadelphia: Westminster Press, 1967) p. 44; John Lachs, "Dogmatist in Disguise," *The Christian Century* 83, no. 46 (November 1966): 1403; Harvey Seifert, "The Promise and Peril of Contextualism," *The Christian Advocate* 10, no. 25 (December 1966): 11; Joseph Mc Cabe, "The Validity of Absolutes," *Commonweal* 73, no. 14 (January 1966): 432-437.

The same difficulty can be see in Robinson. Although he makes more of laws, rules, and objective principles than does Fletcher, yet it is difficult to determine what love would dictate. An example is the Profumo case.

Profumo was a British political official who had been involved in adultery. When accused of this, he lied and then later was compelled to admit his action. A British newspaper suggested that Profumo may have been following Robinson's advice, and was lying to protect his family. Yet, Robinson states unequivocally that this has nothing to do with love, and argues that love would not protect the loved ones from the opportunity to bear the burden and to forgive. Here Robinson definitely makes a moral judgment. What is difficult to discern, however, is the basis of this judgment. Why does love dictate this course of action rather than lying to protect one's family?[10]

The difficulty is more acute when we ask what love means. A definition summarizing the several references might be: love is concern and action for the good or the welfare of the other person. This seems to be implicit in several of Fletcher's statements about love: that it is of people,[11] that it is a way of relating to persons and of using things,[12] that it is good will or benevolence,[13] and that it wills the neighbor's good whether we like him or not.[14]

If love is to serve as our norm and our only norm, it must in some sense indicate what would constitute the good of the other, and what would conduce toward it. Still, Fletcher's principle seems rather vacuous. Basil Mitchell says:

---

10. John Robinson, *Christian Morals Today* (Philadelphia: Westminster Press, 1963), p. 82.

11. Fletcher, *Situation Ethics*, p. 51.

12. Ibid., p. 61.

13. Ibid. pp. 63, 105.

14. Ibid., p. 119.

Professor Fletcher believes that love, and only love, can determine our moral choices. But he does not make it very clear how love does it. . . . Love ensures that the only question before the lover's mind is "What can I do to help?" It does not answer the question. To answer it requires moral insight and to say this is to reopen all the controversies that moral philosophers have engaged in.[15]

But if love is to serve as "norm or measure," certain acts must be ruled out by it at least in the sense that *in a given situation* love indicates what is or is not to be done. Clearly, unless it does so, it cannot provide a guide for action. Love cannot help me to decide between alternatives if any action I might think of doing can, as well as any other, be inspired by love.

Tendency Toward Legalism. Nor is situationism safe from the other extreme, legalism. A good situationist avoids words like "always" and "never." Any action may be either good or bad, depending upon the situation. What is good and right in one situation may well be evil and wrong in another. Nonetheless, both Fletcher and Robinson seem to lapse into universal, or at least very nearly universal, statements. The same is true in less marked degree of the consequentialists.

One of these statements is found in Fletcher's early work, *Morals and Medicine.* Here he seems to endorse the principle that a patient, and particularly a dying patient, has a right to know the truth about his condition. If a physician has a proper understanding of the person and a proper regard for the freedom of a dying person, love will dictate that the patient be told the truth. This seems to be offered as a general rule.[16]

It might be argued that because *Morals and Medicine* was written in 1954, some twelve years before *Situation*

---

15. Basil Mitchell, "Ideals, Roles, and Rules," *Norm and Context in Christian Ethics*, ed. Gene H. Outka and Paul Ramsey (New York: Charles Scribner's Sons), pp. 352-353.

16. Joseph Fletcher, *Morals and Medicine* (Princeton, N.J.: Princeton University Press, 1954), chap. 2.

Ethics, it may represent a presituational period of the development of Fletcher's thought, and that therefore it is unfair to introduce this as inconsistent with his later work. Yet even within *Situation Ethics* there appears to be some inconsistency. He comes close to a categorical statement in his discussion of the girl who is raped while a patient in a mental hospital. His judgment is that "the situationists . . . would almost certainly *in this case* favor abortion and support the girl's father's request."[17] He goes on, however, to support this by an appeal to a principle of considerably greater generality: *"No unwanted and unintended* baby should ever be born."[18] Note the presence of the words "no" and "ever."

A similar phenomenon appears in Robinson's writing:
There are some things of which one may say that it is so inconceivable that they could ever be an expression of love—like cruelty to children or rape—that one might say without much fear of contradiction that they are for Christians always wrong. But they are so persistently wrong *for that reason:* There is not a whole list of things which are sins *per se.*[19]

Robinson feels that the qualifying sentence has preserved the essential principle of his ethical system. What is good is so not because of some quality resident within it but because it embodies love. But the question must be pushed a step further. We must ask why it cannot conceivably be an expression of love. Is there something in the act itself that categorically excludes it from being love?

Indeed, some have challenged this contention, and on situationist grounds. Paul Ramsey suggests a case in which one is commanded to rape a woman.[20] To disobey will result

---

17. Fletcher, *Situation Ethics*, p. 38.

18. Ibid., p. 39.

19. Robinson, *Christian Morals Today*, p. 16.

20. Paul Ramsey, "The Case of the Curious Exception," *Norm and Context in Christian Ethics* ed. Gene H. Outka and Paul Ramsey (New York: Charles Scribner's Sons, 1967), pp. 127-128.

in the woman being killed. Would not the most loving thing be to rape her, if one is an agapeistic situationist, perhaps at least whispering in her ear an explanation of what one is doing? It is difficult to see what objection a situationist could make to this, just as it is difficult to see why the most loving thing to do could not in some cases be to withhold abortion, even if the baby is unwanted and unintended. It might well be replied that in a case such as this, what we have is really not an instance of rape. But that is to raise another important consideration, soon to be dealt with—the matter of the proper description and classification of acts.

Consequentialism attempts to introduce more objective evaluative criteria, by making right and wrong functions of the consequences of the acts. These presumably can be measured by somewhat more scientific methods. But the dilemma remains. Either a certain criterion is set up, generally without justification, as we will see in a later section, or the criteria vary with the individual. In the former case, something of a new legalism arises. In the latter, subjectivism approaching antinomianism is dominant.

These considerations seem to suggest that relativism of the type that we have been examining is an unstable position, tending to lapse either into antinomianism or legalism. Fletcher sharply separated moral decision-making approaches into these three categorical alternatives, and has made them mutually exclusive and exhaustive of the class. It may be that by so doing he has arrived at a stance that cannot be consistently maintained. Perhaps it would be more realistic to conceive of a continuum. Along such a continuum other positions appear, possessing the desirable features pursued by the relativists but without the attendant dilemmas.

Problems of Description and Characterization

The contemporary mood in philosophy lays a heavy emphasis upon semantics. Believing that many of the problems usually wrestled with by philosophers are actually pseudoproblems generated by improper use of language, analytic philosophy proposed to engage in the analysis and rectification of linguistic muddles. Nowhere is this endeavor more important than in ethics. It is the contention of this author that the dilemma faced by these relativists stems in part from confusion or at least ambiguity in the characterization of moral acts.

Consequentialist Description. Fletcher has stated repeatedly that only the end justifies the means. In practice, this seems to involve a collapsing of the distinction between end or genus terms and means, or species terms. This appears in the case of justice. Justice and love become blended.

Paul Ramsey, Eric D'Arcy, J. J. C. Smart, and others have noted that there are numerous ways in which an action may be described.[21] Some actions may properly be described in terms of certain consequences or of certain intentions of the actor. Not all actions can be described in terms of any of their consequences. Thus, suppose that I wish to acquire a certain well-paying and desirable position. This position has definite qualifications, including physical ones, and I find that I am over the weight limit. I go to my doctor and he prescribes a diet, including appetite-suppressing pills. When I take this pill, I may describe the act as follows:

1. I am taking a diet pill.
2. I am suppressing my appetite.
3. I am reducing my food intake.
4. I am lowering my weight.
5. I am qualifying for a job.
6. I am obtaining a better job.
7. I am improving my economic status.
8. I am providing a better life for my family.

Now the problem is this: can description 1 of the act in its most direct or primitive fashion be elided into descriptions 6, 7, or 8? It would seem that there can be an elision into 4, assuming that this is effective toward that end. When we come to the actions farther down the list, however, difficulty begins to emerge. The reason must be sought further.

---

21. Paul Ramsey, *Deeds and Rules in Christian Ethics*, pp. 192-199; Eric D'Arcy, *Human Acts: An Essay on Their Moral Evaluation* (Oxford, England: Oxford University Press, 1963), p. 32.

The example cited may not be as morally relevant as might be desired. Dieting may be a morally neutral or indifferent act. Ramsey, however, cites Smart's case of the Southern sheriff who faces a lynch mob which is about to hang four Negro men chosen at random. The sheriff, an honorable man, sees that the only way to prevent this is to frame one man, whom he knows not to be guilty. There are several ways to describe his action in executing the innocent man:

1. He tensed his forefinger.
2. He pressed a piece of metal.
3. He released a spring.
4. He pulled the trigger of a gun.
5. He fired the gun.
6. He fired a bullet.
7. He shot a bullet at a man.
8. He shot a bullet toward a man.
9. He shot a man.
10. He killed a man.
11. He committed judicial murder.
12. He saved four lives.[22]

Ramsey observes that statement 11 completes the description of the act. Up until this step, one can continue to ask, "What did he *do* then?" After this point, however, one can only ask, "What happened then as a consequence of what he *did?*" "He saved four lives" is a description of the consequence of his action, not of the action itself.[23]

D'Arcy distinguishes between moral-species terms and genus terms. There are, he says, certain moral-species terms where "doing X with the consequence Y" simply cannot be described as "doing Y." There is a cutoff point between the physiological description of the action and the consequentialist description of the action. This distinction must be observed if we want to characterize correctly the actions about which we are speaking.[24]

---

22. D'Arcy, *Human Acts*, p. 3.

23. Ramsey, *Deeds and Rules*, p. 196.

24. D'Arcy, *Human Acts*, p. 32.

In this connection Ramsey notes that situation ethics tends to elide the species term into the generic term. He concedes that it may be legitimate to refer to a case of honest, candid, or loving adultery. It is not appropriate, however, simply to speak of this as a case of honesty, candidness, or love. If he does, Ramsey says that "then one may not have justified the action itself properly termed. He may have only replaced one term needing justification by another that does not in the description of the action."[25] Wherein does the difficulty lie? It seems that the problem comes from the situationist and the consequentialist failing to realize that one cannot describe an action by any and every circumstance. There are, rather, some constituting circumstances and others that are simply extenuating. This means that great care must be taken in properly describing an act, prior to raising the question of its justification.[26]

The difficulty with eliding a species term into a consequence or one of its circumstances is seen when one observes the complexity of the consequences that may flow from an act. Let us take the celebrated case of Mrs. Bergmeier. There are various ways that her action could be characterized. One could simply say, "She was committing adultery." One could also possibly say, "She was reuniting the family." Could you also, however, describe her action by saying, "She was bringing happiness to her family"? If so, then it is at least theoretically imaginable that her action could and should also be described as, "She was creating guilt feelings in herself" or "She was arousing resentment of herself by her husband," or "She was producing feelings of rejection in little Dietrich," or "She was causing the guard to have feelings of self-incrimination," or even "She was contracting venereal disease," or "She was conceiving a baby who would be born blind."

Difficulty results here because a given action may have many different consequences. If in the description of the act,

---

25. Ramsey, *Deeds and Rules*, p. 195.

26. Ibid., p. 197.

it is elided into one of its consequences, only a partial characterization of the act has been given. If it is to be so denominated it ought to be described by the other consequences as well. By eliding a species term into a genus term, the situationist has justified the action. The action, however, is not merely a member of this good genus. It may also be a member of another genus that is not good. Hence, although it could perhaps be said that such an inclusion is a correct designation of the act, it is not the only morally relevant consideration regarding that act. Whereas the generic designation may indicate a class of good actions, insofar as they are members of the class, not all members are the same. One of the important factors distinguishing among the members may be that some are also members of other generic classes. It would seem that less confusion would be introduced if instead of eliding the description of act X into "He did Y," it were restricted to the actual act, "He did X, with the consequence Y."

It is important to remember the distinction between constituting and nonconstituting circumstances of an act. It appears that Fletcher's method rests upon an internal contradiction. On the one hand, many actions are justified by redescribing them in terms of a generic title. On the other, much of the leverage gained against absolutism, legalism, and intrinsicalism derives from retaining the original designation, even in a sensationalistic fashion.

Thus, he does not attempt to answer the charge that raising euthanasia to a general line of action would be harmful. Rather, he redescribes it as "loving-kindness," and states the objector's position as being that "a particular case of loving-kindness, *if everybody did it*, would mean chaos and cruelty" (italics his).[27]

Similarly, any possible conflict between justice and love is disposed of by describing justice as love distributed.[28] Further, when T. E. Lawrence killed Hamed the Moor, he

---

27. Fletcher, *Situation Ethics*, p. 130.

28. Ibid., chap. 5.

apparently was not committing murder or manslaughter; he was ending the conflict and quelling the bloodletting.[29] Ramsey also feels that what is entailed in the vast scale of "agapeic calculus" that led President Truman to the decision to use the A-bombs on Hiroshima and Nagasaki is a redescription of his action as "saving lives on the beaches of Japan."[30] He was, of course, doing much else besides.

The Dialectic of Definition. Yet there is a dialectic in Fletcher's method, whereby the original, rather sensationalistic designation is retained. Having indicated in one place that taking a revolver from a homicidal maniac is not stealing (it is presumably loving-kindness),[31] he nonetheless speaks later of stealing a man's gun to keep him from shooting someone in anger.[32] Fletcher would no doubt reply that the two situations are different. It would seem, however, that if two such similar cases must be considered as different, the danger of falling into antinomianism again reasserts itself. The action of Mother Maria who chose to die in a gas chamber in place of a young ex-Jewish girl is described as suicide but also as "sacrificing her life on the model of Christ."[33] Thus, by presumably redescribing her action as an instance of sacrificial loving-kindness he justifies it, while by retaining the designation "suicide" he shows that suicide may sometimes be right. The question, however, is whether sacrificing one's life for the sake of others ought to be (and whether indeed it is by competent moralists) described as suicide. Jesus commended it as the ultimate instance of love (John 15:13) and even engaged in it Himself. Is this, however, to be assimilated to other cases that all agree

---

29. Ibid., p. 98.

30. Ramsey, *Deeds and Rules*, p. 201.

31. Fletcher, *Situation Ethics*, p. 59.

32. Ibid., p. 125.

33. Ibid., p. 74.

are suicide? Is there no difference between the act of a soldier who throws himself on a live grenade to spare the lives of his comrades and that of a person who jumps off a bridge because of sorrow in love or failure in business?

Additional instances can be produced. The plot to kill Hitler, in which Bonhoeffer was involved, is described as "murder." [34] If that act is justified, then presumably murder cannot be held to be universally and intrinsically wrong. The question, however, is whether this is a case of murder. He speaks of surgeons *mutilating* bodies to remove cancers, and of nurses *lying* to schizophrenics to keep them calmer for treatment.[35] Judith, in the apocryphal book of that name, is spoken of as *"lying"* to Holofernes, "using her sex. . . *whoringly* in order to *murder* him" (italics added). Yet what she did is also redescribed as "saving the people Israel."[36] It appears that the use of more technical descriptive terms, such as "homicide" and "seductively," would contribute more to the rational resolution of the moral dilemmas that are involved than do terms like "murder" and "whoringly."[37]

Confusion of Generality and Specificity. It begins to appear that Fletcher may not be playing according to the rules of the game of polemics. For example, in his effort to point up the vulnerability of universal and unexceptionable laws, he seems to assume that universal laws must be of the maximum level of generality, and if an exception to such an abstract universal is found, law has been rebutted. The fact that in many cases he can find exceptions to very general laws seems to support his contention that nothing is always right and good (except love). Note, however, that a law may be much more complex than simply "A is always wrong,"

---

34. Ibid., p. 33.

35. Ibid., p. 123.

36. Ibid., p. 66.

37. Ramsey, *Deeds and Rules*, p. 206.

and still possess the qualities of law and of universality. Fletcher seems to assume that if he has found a case X where A is not wrong, he has overthrown legalism, universals, and intrinsicalism. The law, however, may actually be "A is always wrong except when X is present, in which case A is right." Similarly, in a case of Y where A is wrong, this second formulation of law may not have been overturned either. It may simply be the case that the further elaboration of the law should actually read, "A is always wrong except when X is present *and Y is not present*, in which case A is right." Thus a case of XY does not violate the law.

Now it may be charged that this series of qualifications of the originally formulated law can be continued indefinitely, so that finally all laws are so closely defined that they pertain to classes having only one member. This of course would be the opposite extreme from laws being of maximum generality. It should be noted, however, that failure to adhere to one extreme does not necessarily require going to the other.

Use of Unrepresentative Examples. The instances of legalism cited are often rather poor examples. An example is the English law that a marriage must be validated by a sexual union.[38] A case arose where a couple because of a temporary physiological problem had been unable thus to consummate their marriage. The wife had conceived a child by artificial insemination from her husband. This meant that the husband was physically the father of the child. It was his sperm that had fertilized the ovum. Yet, true to the law, the court ruled that the man and woman were not legally married and the child was illegitimate. This seems to be held up as evidence against legalism or law in any of its forms, since Fletcher terms it an illustration of what legalism does in the civil order.

Many moralists who maintain that it is meaningful to speak of laws, objective principles, and norms, would merely

---

38. Fletcher, *Situation Ethics*, pp. 78-79.

say that this is a poor, unwise, and foolish law. The existence of a bad instance does not in itself argue for or against the principle of objectivity or normativity of moral judgments.

Ad Hominem *Argument and Pejorative Language.* The use of disparagingly descriptive terms accentuates Fletcher's frequent employment of *ad hominem* argument to make this point. This is seen in the numerous examples of pejorative language: "encumbered with a whole apparatus of prefabricated rules and regulations;"[39] "tricky and tortuous now-you-see-it, now-you-don't business . . . hair-splitting and logic-chopping study of the letter of the law."[40] All legalists are lumped together as wanting "to lean on strong, unyielding rules," or "wallow and cower in the security of the law."[41] He refers to the "ethical establishment," "a growing hunger for law," "a neurotic security device to simplify moral decisions," [42] and "childish rules."[43] In addition to being rather questionable tactics, such use of emotion-laden language scarcely contributes to calm rational resolution.

The Extreme Case as the Norm. Further, the cases to which Fletcher appeals are frequently very extreme cases. He undoubtedly is trying to make the point that there are cases in which the particular law does not apply. Having, however, established to his satisfaction that the law does not apply in this extreme instance, he then seems ready to move to other much less unusual cases, applying the same thinking.[44] The

---

39. Ibid., p. 18.

40. Ibid., pp. 18-19.

41. Ibid., p. 134.

42. Ibid., p. 132.

43. Ibid., p. 40.

44. Harmon L. Smith, review in *The Duke Divinity School Review* (Spring 1966). Reprinted in Harvey Cox, ed., *The Situation Ethics Debate* (Philadelpha: Westminster Press, 1968), p. 98.

assumption apparently is that whatever law was believed to govern the one case governs the other.

For example, if the rule is "Sexual intercourse is to be engaged in only within the bounds of marriage," then Mrs. Bergmeier's case might perhaps be regarded as an annulling or exceptionable case. One might argue that here was a truly desperate situation, a forced choice in which the need of her family dictated this action. What about the young couple, however, who want to be married and whose parents object? Fletcher says that they might decide to have intercourse, getting the girl pregnant to coerce the parents into granting their permission.[45] This would seem to be quite a different matter. Here it appears that the situation is much less urgent, the choice less forced. Similarly, it is one thing to discuss the propriety of abortion for the schizophrenic rape victim in a mental hospital; it is quite a different matter to assert that no unwanted and unintended baby should ever be born.[46]

Problems of Assessment of the Moral Predicament

All of what has gone before can be subsumed under one general heading: inaccuracy of description or analysis in moral discourse. The other major cluster of difficulties lies in what might be termed unreality of assessment of the moral predicament.

Great Amount of Information Needed. The situationists seem to reckon inadequately with the great complexity of issues involved and the enormous amount of information required to make moral decisions situationally. Mrs. Bergmeier, if she is to decide upon sacrificial adultery, must attempt to calculate the effects of her action upon the family as a whole: herself, her husband, little Dietrich, and even the guard. How can she possibly have enough knowledge and insight to work out all of this and reach a decision?

---

45. Fletcher, *Situation Ethics*, p. 104.

46. Ibid., pp. 37-39.

There is a sense in which the context of decision is the whole of society and the entire span of present and future time. Mrs. Bergmeier must take into account Dietrich's future wife and children (if any), the present and future family of the guard, and many other persons and circumstances. There is a law in physics that to every action there is an equal and opposite reaction. If I stand on the earth and jump, the earth also moves. The movement is so very slight as to be negligible, but it is there nonetheless. Similarly, when I perform a moral act, at least potentially the entire moral universe moves.

The consequentialists also make crucial decisions on the basis of what necessarily must be incomplete inductions. Inherent in the nature of inductive inquiry is the fact that the induction must generally stop at some point short of 100 percent induction. This means that there is always an element of uncertainty in the conclusions that are drawn. Yet in many cases, irreversible decisions are being made.

Particularly is this true since many of the possible consequences may not appear until some time quite far in the future. For example, if one decides to use the hallucinogenic drugs because they do not appear to have any adverse effects, he is basing his decision on data that is incomplete, since no very long period of observation has been available thus far.

The other problem is that there are often many consequences of an action rather than one. The problem of "undesirable side effects" is a real one, yet it seems to be neglected by many of these writers. The assumption that premarital sex is not wrong is maintained by showing that the triple fears of infection, detection, and pregnancy are no longer problems. But are these the only possible consequences of premarital coitus? Consideration of other "by-products," including later guilt feelings and the effect upon relationships with other persons such as one's parents, is largely neglected.

Can a finite human being gather sufficient data and calculate accurately enough to determine what really is the most loving thing to do or determine the course of action leading to the best consequences? Fletcher recognizes this problem but passes it by, apparently on the basis that one has no other option but to act, difficult as the situation is. Another alternative would seem to be the possibility that some omniscient being, capable of assessing and calculating all the factors, might reveal the solution. This possibility, which will form the basis of the argument in the next chapter, seems to be automatically excluded or at least ignored by those who propound the theories that we are examining.

Neglect of Long-Range Factors. Closely related to this first tendency is a second. The emphasis in these discussions seems to be upon short-range considerations, to the virtual avoidance of long-range issues.[47] When consequences are evaluated, it is the immediate situation that is considered. Alleviating of an immediate problem, rather than consideration of the ramifications of the proposed solution, seems to be paramount. This is true, even when the long-range possibilities can be known or at least anticipated. In the Mrs. Bergmeier case, no consideration seems to be given to the question of the future effects upon the relationship between Mr. and Mrs. Bergmeier, such as the future guilt feelings that she may experience or the resentment that he may feel toward his wife. Similarly, no question is raised how little Dietrich's self-image may be affected when he discovers how he came to be conceived. Although this is indeed the now generation, we must seriously ask whether such omission really is responsible.

Ignoring of Unresolved Issues. There is in some ways a seeming naivete or lack of sensitivity to the difficulties or a lack of real wrestling with unresolved problems.[48] For

---

47. Joseph F. Green, review in the February 1966 release of the Sunday School Board of the Southern Baptist Convention. Reprinted in *The Situation Ethics Debate*, p. 78; James M. Gustafson, "How Does Love Reign?" *The Christian Century* 83, no. 18 (May 1966): 654.

48. Smith, *Situation Ethics Debate*, p. 96.

example, in the consideration of possible abortion, one of the issues that presumably must be grappled with is the question of whether an unborn embryo is a human life—a person, and if so, at what point is it to be identified as such. This is no small problem, and a great deal of study and soul-searching has been engaged in by various persons in this connection.[49] Yet both Fletcher and the consequentialists seem to blithely assume that the embryo is not a person or a human life at this stage. Such unsupported and virtually unqualified assumptions are reminiscent of the legalism that they so steadfastly oppose.

Lack of Ultimate Criteria. We noted earlier the problem of vagueness of the concept of love in the situationist statements. It appears that a similar problem is also present in the consequentialists' theory. We have observed the comment of Milhaven that what has occurred here is a shift from an ethic of principles to an ethic of experience.[50] These experiences are the data for determining whether the consequences of one action are preferable to those of another. The problem, however, lies in the question of normativity of experience, or to put it differently, the criteria by which experiences are to be judged.

Let us say, for example, that a question such as legalization of hallucinogenic drugs were under consideration. Data from social scientists and medical doctors would be scrutinized to determine what the results of such a step would be. The decision then would be made in terms of which course of action would have better consequences for man. The problem, however, is to determine what is good for man. What is his end, his real life? What is man? To judge

---

49. Cf. the several articles in an entire issue of *Christianity Today* 13, no. 3 (November 1968), devoted to the subject of contraception and abortion. These papers were read at a symposium convened by the Christian Medical Society in Portsmouth, New Hampshire, the last week of August 1968.

50. John G. Milhaven, "The Abortion Debate: An Epistemological Interpretation," *Theological Studies* 31, no. 1 (March 1970): 114-115.

what is loving for man or what are good consequences requires a considerable ideological apparatus. No such anthropology is discussed by Fletcher, and it is certainly not explicit in the consequentialists' writings, either.

The understanding of man must be placed in a broader conceptual system as well. If man is primarily a biological creature, then certain consequences will be the best for him. If, on the other hand, he is a creature intended for eternal fellowship with God, then other consequences will be the most desirable. In turn, the nature and end of man will be determined or at least affected by one's view of God. If God is a very holy God, who punishes sin with everlasting punishment, man's situation is quite different than it would be if God is indulgent and willing to overlook deviations from His will. Fletcher, however, seems to summarize his doctrine of God by simply saying that God is "personal" and has created men in His own image.[51] As a result, personality is deemed a first-order concern in ethical choices; yet this itself is also a rather vague concept. Elsewhere he says that situation ethics has nothing to do with Christian theology in a special way.[52] This is an inadequate basis for determining in a given case what the good for man (in which love demands should be sought) would be.

Those who base their judgment of rightness and wrongness of actions on their consequences also do not appear to be working with a very explicit conception of man. Without this it is very difficult to pass judgment on an action in terms of its consequences. It is like a race in which once the runners begin running, the finish line is removed. After a few laps, virtually any runner could be judged to be leading the race, since he appears to be ahead of several others. Without some fixed reference point, however, there is no way really to judge who is the winner. This appears to be the case here, as well.

---

51. Fletcher, *Situation Ethics*, p. 51.

52. Ibid., pp. 14-15.

Lack of Awareness of the Brokenness of Life. There also seems to be in the situation ethics that we have been studying a lack of real awareness of the depth of tragedy or brokenness of life. If it is necessary to kill persons to do the loving thing (the best thing for the greatest number of persons), then this is not only right—it is also good. It is not a necessary evil or the lesser of two evils. It is apparent that what Fletcher is trying to combat is the guilty conscience sometimes possessed by those who have honestly tried to do their very best. Yet there are some of us who might kill, if necessary, to accomplish some other good, yet who would do so with a sense of real remorse. It would be with the regret that the present world is one in which there is no better alternative than this.[53] No doubt this is simply an instance of the intrinsicalist thinking that Fletcher so sternly denies. It would seem that many people, including the modern man whom these relativists admire so, have difficulty in thinking of the deliberate taking of human life as really being "good." Witness the widespread liberal reaction against the Indo-China War and capital punishment. It is the labeling of taking of human life as "good" that has led some critics to refer to Fletcher as cold-blooded. There does not seem to be sufficient recognition of the fact that a course of action, while being best overall, may not be the best or the most loving for each person involved.

Naivete Regarding the Goodness of Man. Closely related to this is an apparent assumption about the ability of man to recognize the truth. Reinhold Niebuhr has described original sin as the tendency of the self to be more concerned with itself than to be embarrassed by its undue claims and pretensions.[54] This is confirmed in the observation that most

---

53. James M. Gustafson, "How Does Love Reign?"; Charles E. Curran, "Dialogue With Joseph Fletcher," *The Homiletic and Pastoral Review* 67, no. 10 (July 1967): 829.

54. Reinhold Niebuhr, *The Self and the Dramas of History* (London: Faber and Faber, 1956), p. 30.

persons tend to favor themselves and that scarcely anyone believes that in differences of opinion with another person he has not been right more than half of the time. Yet in the relativistic ethical views that we have been studying there is apparently no real place given to original sin and its effect upon one's judgment in calculating what is loving.[55]

The difficulty of making one's decision in the situation ("then and there") is also apparently underestimated. If situationism involves a careful, shrewd calculation, then the immediate situation may not present the most favorable circumstances in which to do the calculation. There may be insufficient time available, for one thing. Further, there may not be access to all of the pertinent data required for a critical decision. Finally, there may be emotional involvement that would distort the judgment. A young unmarried couple in a parked car on a dark side road, for example, may find it difficult to calculate coolly and rationally what is the most agapeic thing to do. There is great danger that *eros* will overwhelm *agape* in such a situation. It would seem that weighing the factors in advance would potentially make for a more objective decision in some instances; yet Fletcher steadfastly rejects any attempt to propound "prefabricated" solutions.[56]

There also appears to be unwarranted optimism with regard to man's ability to do the good. The assumption evidently is that knowing what is right and wanting to do it is all that is really required. Yet numerous Christians find that the personal experience of Paul is also theirs: "I can will what is right, but I cannot do it. For I do not do the good I want, but the evil I do not want is what I do" (Romans 7:18b–19, RSV).

In one of the churches where this author served as

---

55. Robert E. Fitch, "The Protestant Sickness," *Religion in Life* 35, no. 4 (Autumn 1966): 499; C. Peter Wagner, "Is Love Enough?" *Eternity* 18, no. 2 (February 1967): 59.

56. Elton M. Eenigenberg, "How New Is the New Morality?" *The Reformed Review* 20, no. 3 (March 1967): 11-23.

pastor, the young people of the church wanted to put on a play during the Christmas holiday vacation period. One of the ladies in the church wrote a play and asked the pastor to criticize the script. The story was set in the 1980s. The world powers had built forces and tensions to a danger point where world population destruction, particularly by Red China, was a grave threat. The leaders of the nations agreed to a procedure to resolve the tensions. They would take the wisdom of all the greatest religious and philosophical thinkers of all time and feed it into a computer. The computer would present a solution, which these world leaders had previously bound themselves to follow. The world waited anxiously as the computer assimilated all of the data and finally delivered its verdict: "Love one another." End of play.

The young pastor wrote a comment in the margin: "You have not given a satisfying conclusion to the play. This is not the answer; this is the problem." To know that one ought to love is one thing. To be able to love is another, and this is the exceedingly difficult part. The cognizance of just how difficult this is does not seem to be fully present in the writings of these relativists.

This is the place where grace and divine enablement ought to be emphasized. One could expect that Christian ethics would lay particular stress upon the need of daily dependence upon God for assistance in fulfilling the demands of life. Nor would it be out of place to anticipate that there would even be entreaty to God for the remaking of the moral character of the subject himself (orthodox Christian theology speaks of regeneration and sanctification). There is a strange scarcity of reference to this in the writings of Fletcher and Robinson and in the Lutheran and Presbyterian statements.[57] Grace enters into Fletcher's ethic largely in terms of forgiveness for failure to achieve the good and particularly to discern the good.

---

57. Henlee H. Barnette, *The New Theology and Morality* (Philadelphia: Westminster Press, 1967), p. 47. "Lutheran Sex Code: Covenant Above Contract," *Christianity Today* 14, no. 22 (July 1970): 32-33. Jack Star, "The Presbyterian Debate Over Sex, *Look*, 11 August 1970, pp. 54ff.

Subsumption of the First Great Commandment. Indeed, God seems to be neglected in other respects as well. The command to love derives from Jesus' statement that we are to love our neighbor as ourselves; but this is made the sole norm. It should be noted that this was, according to Jesus, the *second* command. The first was: "You shall love the Lord your God with all your heart, and with all your soul, and with all your mind, and with all your strength" (Mark 12:30). This, however, receives strikingly little attention.[58] With all of the emphasis upon love being expressed for all persons, the one person almost invariably overlooked is the supreme person—God. Jesus (who in the orthodox interpretation believed and claimed Himself to be God just as the Father) said, "If you love me, you will keep my commandments" (John 14:15, RSV). While He went on to say, "This is my commandment, that you love one another as I have loved you" (John 15:12), it is evident that this was not His only commandment. In effect the situationist seems to say that the way we love God is by loving other men, and this particularly fits Robinson's doctrine of God.[59] Whereas Jesus did speak of this possibility (Matthew 25:31-46), He did not simply reduce loving God to loving other men. Indeed, there are suggestions in Scripture of instances where these two might be antithetical to one another (cf., Acts 4:19).

Failure to Consider Divine Providence. The providence of God does not really seem to influence the calculations, either. The possibility that God might supernaturally intervene in ways that could not be merely naturalistically predicted or anticipated does not appear to be considered. Suppose that it is God's will for Mrs. Bergmeier to refrain from adultery. Is it not possible that God might yet return

---

58. C. Peter Wagner, "Is Love Enough?" *Eternity* 18, no. 2 (February 1967): 59.

59. Fletcher, *Situation Ethics*, pp. 155, 156, 158; John A. T. Robinson, *Honest to God* (Philadelphia: Westminster Press, 1963), chap. 5.

her to her family by some means not presently predictable? Or if He allows her to remain in the prison, might He not sustain the family even without her?

The Presbyterian statement points out the earlier sexual maturity of young people today, but also the deferred date of marriage in our society. This means that greater pressures are put upon young people with respect to sex drives. If this is so, should not the possibility of Paul's suggestion regarding divine enablement in the face of temptation be considered (as in I Corinthians 10:13)? In these areas, faith in God ought to make a difference. Instead, there seems to be in practice something of a naturalistic bias at work.

Oversight of Other Alternatives. Closely related to this is the tendency to set up two alternatives as exhausting the possibilities while overlooking any other human solutions.[60] For example, in the case of Holmes in the lifeboat, are there no other possibilities besides everyone remaining in the boat and all perishing or Holmes casting the men into the sea? Although the men had refused to leave the boat, might there not have been some method remaining, such as drawing lots, to see who would leap overboard? If someone declined to agree to such a procedure or refused to cooperate when he saw that his lot was drawn, at least the majority could presumably have enforced the rule, taking some of the responsibility off Holmes. In any event, this is a possibility that ought logically to be considered.[61] Similarly, with the young engaged couple whose parents refused to grant permission for them to marry, the possibility of waiting until both were of age and the parents' permission would not be required seems to be overlooked as a viable alternative.

Neglect of the Role of Binding Relationships. There also does not seem to be adequate attention given to certain relationships or binding commitments that may alter situa-

---

60. Barnette, *The New Theology and Morality*, p. 46.

61. Ramsey, *Deeds and Rules*, p. 217.

tions.[62] Take, for example, the case of the man who is able to rescue only one man from a fire and must choose between his father and a scientist who has discovered a cure for cancer.[63] An inclination toward rescuing his father in this case might stem from mere sentiment, of course. On the other hand, it might flow from certain responsibilities or obligations that are involved in the parent-child relationship. It may be that something is owed to the father, *because he is the father*, which is not owed to anyone else. This dimension does not seem to enter into the calculation.

The difficulty shows itself again when Fletcher says, "It is right to deal lovingly with the enemy *unless to do so hurts too many friends.*"[64] What he does not tell us, however, is how many is too many. Does it take one more friend than enemy to make too many, or may a fewer number of friends than enemies still be too many? When he says that "the enemy-neighbor has no stronger claims than a friend-neighbor, after all," there is an implication that he has no less a claim either.

Excessive Individualism. The consequentialists in particular appear to this writer to have adopted an overly individualistic approach, in which the fabric of social relationships receives relatively little emphasis. This is particularly evident with respect to the marriage ceremony.

To be sure, the heart of the marriage relationship is a personal commitment of two individuals to one another on a permanent basis. It is true that this pledge of faithfulness is what really unites them, and without this a legal ceremony by the state means relatively little. Nonetheless, the function of the public ceremony introduces significant values.

---

62. Ibid., p. 163, Donald Evans, "Love, Situations and Rules," *Norm and Context in Christian Ethics* ed. Gene Outka and Paul Ramsey (New York: Charles Scribner's Sons, 1967), pp. 383-389.

63. Fletcher, *Situation Ethics*, p. 115.

64. Ibid.

Public legal marriage involves other persons in the relationship as witnesses to the resolve of these two people. In the Christian understanding of marriage, the role goes beyond that of witnesses. When two members of the body of Christ pledge themselves to one another in the presence of other believers, there is an implicit promise on the part of these other members of the body of a supportive role. There is a covenant to pray for this couple for the fulfillment of their marriage vows. There are other supportive functions as well, such as encouragement, counsel, and actual assistance.

The process of application for a marriage license, with the filing and recording of the certificate and the attendant publicity, serves to give the widest possible notice that, as the Bible puts it, the man has forsaken father and mother and is joined to his wife (Genesis 2:24). The rite of circumcision established unmistakably that the proselyte had been converted to the Hebrew faith and united to the community of the Hebrew nation. The Christian convert is baptized as a public sign of his commitment to follow Christ. In non-Christian cultures, this is regarded as a very significant sign indeed. Similarly, the public marriage may serve a very vital role in the stability of that relationship.

In this connection, it appears that these relativists overlook certain positive values of law. Law tends to be regarded here as something of a hardship to be endured, a burden that society imposes upon the individual. No possibility is entertained that law can be a help that society provides. Assuming the value of the depth of commitment involved in a permanent or long-term relationship, it seems that law may be of valuable assistance to this process.

Every human relationship is subject to certain strains and difficulties. This is certainly true in marriage where differences of taste and opinion arise. In this situation, the type of relationship required by merely a private understanding can be severed fairly easily. Where a legal marriage exists, however, a termination is not so easily effected. It means that the persons must "think twice" before severing the bond. This "cooling-off" period is frequently helpful in maintaining the relationship. Indeed, where two persons antecedently understand the significance of this relationship and the difficulty of dissolving it, there should be a more careful initiation of the experience with a consequent greater depth.

Improper Use of the Bible. A further fault is involved in the way the Bible is employed. Here the criticism does not concern insufficient or excessive use of the Bible nor the correct or incorrect use of it, but rather that it is used *arbitrarily.* In other words, the impression is left that the conclusion has already been determined and that an interpretation is sought and accepted that will agree with this preset conclusion. This is commonly known as rationalization, and it can employ the Bible as well as any other means to its end.

Fletcher, for example, uses Paul's "all things are lawful for me, but not all things are helpful" (taken out of context), yet ignores statements such as "do not let what is good to you be spoken of as evil," and "if food is a cause of my brother's falling, I will never eat meat" (I Corinthians 6:12; Romans 14:16; I Corinthians 8:13, RSV).

Treese's discussion of homosexuality examines a number of biblical passages. Yet the conclusions seem somewhat preset. His exegesis of the incident at Sodom and Gomorrah, for example, suggests the possibility that the word "know" may simply mean "get acquainted with" in this instance.[65] Yet if this was the meaning intended, evidently Lot misunderstood, since his actions seem to indicate that he believed the men of the city had something more in mind than just a social visit. When Treese finds certain passages of the New Testament that rather unequivocally reject homosexuality, he dismisses these by simply indicating that Scripture as a whole must be judged by contemporary experience.[66]

---

65. Robert L. Treese, "Homosexuality: A Contemporary View of the Biblical Perspective" (Paper prepared for the Consultation on Theology and the Homosexual, sponsored by the Glide Urban Center and the Council on Religion and the Homosexual in San Francisco, August 22-24, 1966), pp 8-12.

66. Ibid., p. 18.

Failure to Distinguish Between Persons and Actions. Both the situationists and their heirs, the consequentialists, have insisted that ethics be centered upon persons rather than laws, rules, or principles. When this is done, however, one result seems to be an inability to distinguish between the person as a person and his actions.

This may be seen in Treese's consideration of homosexuality. He observes that many homosexuals whom he has known bore evidence of the grace of God. These people display marks of the Holy Spirit in them. It is apparent that they have been accepted by God. They should also, therefore, be accepted by God's people.[67] Yet he seems to suggest that this means the actions of the person are similarly legitimate. At least there is no intimation that the homosexuality of the individual is to be considered a sin or even a sickness, of which the person either needs to repent or be cured. Is this really the idea that acceptance of an individual as a person also means condoning whatever he does? If this is the case, then it would also work in reverse; disapproval of the actions of a person would entail rejection of the person himself.

Confusion of Being and Knowing. There appears to be a confusion of being and knowing, ontology and epistemology. This is particularly marked in the thought of Fletcher. The argument against there being some type of absolutes or norms at times seems to stem from inability to determine the facts. Fletcher cites the case of the destroyer commander in Monsarrat's *The Cruel Sea.*[68] The commander must decide whether to drop a depth charge in an attempt to destroy an enemy submarine deep in the water. If he does, he will surely kill hundreds of seamen who are already in the sea, but he may get the U-boat. If he does not, the men will not immediately perish and may well be rescued, but the enemy submarine may sink additional ships, killing other men. The

---

67. Ibid., pp 24-25, 32.

68. Ibid., p. 152.

difficulty is that he really does not know the location of the submarine. If he did, and could know whether he would be able to destroy it, there might well be agreement that this is the right thing to do. Some of the force of Fletcher's argument throughout the book appears to derive from confusing "We do not know the norm" with "there is no norm."

The Problem of Moral Instruction. A potential problem also attaches to the utility of situation ethics for moral instruction or catechizing of children. Whereas the situational method of following the dictates of love alone might be sufficient for the mature adult, how will moral instruction be effected with the child unless there are objective guidelines?[69] There is a practical problem here that probably extends well beyond childhood.

---

69. John M. Swomley, Jr., in Harvey Cox, ed., *The Situation Ethics Debate* (Philadelphia: Westminster Press, 1968), pp. 90-91; Eenigenberg, "How New is the New Morality?" p. 23.

5

An
Alternative Approach

We have seen in the previous chapter that relative ethics has numerous and serious faults. It is not sufficient, however, to point out the shortcomings of a view. Intellectual responsibility requires that some constructive alternative be presented. An insight from John Baillie is appropriate here. Baillie had written a paper in which he had extensively and effectively criticized a particular theory. The professor's comment written on the paper was simple but telling: "Every theory has difficulties, but you have not considered whether any other theory has less difficulties than the one you have criticized."[1] This is a point well taken.

What follows will not be an exhaustive development of an ethic. Rather, it is more nearly an outline or an agenda. The developing of a system would require a separate treatment. Here we will attempt to incorporate what seem to this writer to be valid insights in relativism while avoiding its weaknesses and flaws.

THE ONTOLOGICAL BASIS
OF MORAL JUDGMENTS

There are a number of areas that need to be explored. The first concerns the ontological basis of moral judgments. It appears to this observer that a large part of Fletcher's

---

1. John Baillie, *Invitation to Pilgrimage* (New York: Charles Scribner's Sons, 1942), p. 15.

difficulty stems from his antimetaphysical approach. He is careful to avoid reifying "good." It has substantive status only in God. Good is not inherent in or intrinsic to any objects. Even the exact status of love or good in God is somewhat unclear. An effort is made to maintain as nearly as possible a purely pragmatic approach to ethics. Unless there is some definite status for good, however, it is very difficult to recognize it. What is good, and what is there within an object of value that makes it good? Where does good reside? If good is to be more than simply a designation that men attach to an object, what is its status? Is there anything in the structure of reality that makes things good or that counts for good?

Good as the Will of God

The beginning point or the basic premise of this approach will be the tenet that there exists a God: an all-wise, all-powerful, and personal being. He is the creator of all that is. Everything derives from Him, whether objects, living beings, or values. He not only has brought the creation into being, but He preserves it and directs it. He is the supreme being. There is nothing higher in the universe to which to appeal.

This is a fundamental assumption. It is, as Fletcher would say, posited rather than discovered. It is not antecedently proved by anything else. It is a basic starting point. Once made, however, it can be validated. The presupposition of this supreme being is taken from the assertion of the Bible, which claims to be a revelation or manifestation of God's mind and will. Its validation can be measured by a twofold test. On the one hand, its internal consistency and coherence, and, on the other hand, its external adequacy in accounting accurately for a wide span of experience argue for its validity as a world-and-life view. To engage in a treatment of this principle in the several areas of experience would go beyond the scope of this chapter. It is hoped that its superiority in the area of ethical experience will be exhibited.

Good, in this view, is that which God wills. Since He is the highest object, this cannot be defined by anything else.

The nature of what God wills can be described by observing some of the specifics that He wills, but these are good as a consequence of His willing it.

This means that God does not will something because it is good. There is not some antecedent or independent factor that God discovers and wills because He is bound to it and must conform. It is good because He has chosen to look with favor upon it. Were there some higher standard to which even God is answerable then He would in effect not really be God.

God's Will as Expression of His Nature.

This is not arbitrary, however. Although God does not will on the basis of external criteria, He does choose consistently with His nature. Thus, ultimately God's will is an expression of His nature. This should not be construed as a lack of freedom, for freedom is not a mere sporadic absence of limitation of any type. Freedom is the absence of external restraint, not the ability to act inconsistently with one's nature. This is to say that God could not have been other than He is. He could not have been capable of what we call cruelty or untruthfulness or any of several other negative qualities. He cannot will to tell a lie or to break His word.

Situationism makes much of love as its sole principle or guide in ethics. It does this on the basis that God's nature is love and that this one place where love is substantive makes it the pattern for human action. This is true, for the Bible says, "God is love." Fletcher's most biblical chapter is the one entitled, "Loving Is Not Liking." Here he develops very well the biblical concept of *agape*, not as a sentimental feeling or pleasant attitude toward the other person, but as concern for the welfare of the other, which shows itself in action aimed at attaining that welfare.

At the same time, however, it should be noted that love is not the only attribute of God nor the whole of His nature. It appears that situationism of the Fletcherian variety treats the statement "God is love" as a statement of equivalency, or identity. On this basis, "God is love" is virtually a definition. A closer examination of the Bible, however, suggests that it is instead a statement of predication. This makes love one of God's characteristics or attributes, but without excluding the possibility of there being others as well.

Specifically, the Bible attributes holiness and moral righteousness to God. He does not simply do good to man. He makes demands or requirements of man. He expects man to be pure as He is, to abstain from certain actions that He identifies as wrong. This is an aspect of God's nature that is as prominent in the Bible as is His love.

There is not a tension within the personality of God, however. The love of God is love that is consonant with, or is tempered by, His holiness. His holiness, by the same measure, is always informed by His love. Seeing this additional attribute (plus others as well) enables one to correctly apprehend God's love rather than forming a one-sided, unbalanced idea.

This means that careful attention must be given to the priority of commands found in the Bible. The command to love one's neighbor as himself is only the second command-ment. Ahead of it comes the first and great commandment, to love God with all of one's being. This ethic is not primarily humanistic in the sense that humanism makes man the highest object of value. God is superior to this, and the first consideration is that He be properly respected, honored, and glorified. In part, this means that the question of obedience to God's commands is prior to love to one's fellowman.

Jesus pointed out (John 14:15, 21, 23, 24) that a claim of loving God is virtually meaningless apart from obeying His commands. This is the primary way of demonstrating love. Where this is absent, the profession of love for Him is of dubious value and significance.

This is not a matter of slavish submission to a powerful tyrant, however. Jesus told His disciples that they were not servants (literally, "slaves"). They were now His friends. It is a matter of a friend doing what his friend desires, simply to please him (John 15:14, 15).

God's Will as Based upon Perfect and Complete Knowledge

God, when He wills, is capable of foreseeing all of the

consequences and implications, for He is omniscient. He knows all things intuitively, or without having to calculate and deduce. Thus when He wills something, He is able to take account of all the variables, to measure the effect that this will have not only upon a few persons living now, but upon all persons at all times present and future and in all circumstances. Further, He is all-powerful, capable, if He chooses, of bringing about His will and of demanding and enforcing such conformity.

God's will should be thought of as His most ultimate desires and intentions. It should be noted that there may sometimes be a difference or distinction that can be drawn between this and His actual decisions. Thus God sometimes may choose to allow a person to do something that is contrary to His wish or desire or ultimate will. This may have the effect of bringing the person to a realization of the undesirability of his action and cause him to conform to God's will in the ultimate sense. The perfectly good would, however, be reserved as a designation of the former meaning of the will of God.

On this basis, the question of good resolves into the issue of whether the action in question agrees with God's will. If so, it is good; if not, it is less than fully good.

This means that an objective basis is given to ethical statements. Good is not simply what is esteemed by a man (which may be quite different from what the next man esteems). It is what God says it is, irrespective of man's opinion. It is not dependent upon recognition or acceptance by men.

The problem of ethics then becomes a comparatively simple (although not an easy) one. It is a function of one question: "Does this idea or this proposed course of action coincide with the will of God, or does it more closely approximate God's will than do any of the alternatives?"

THE EPISTEMOLOGY OF CHRISTIAN ETHICS

This means that the second and major issue of this Christian ethic will be epistemological. If we have determined the definition of good, the next question is how we know what is God's will and how we verify our claim to having knowledge of that will.

This approach rests its case upon a doctrine of revelation, both general and special. God has made known to man something of His nature and His will. It is a matter of studying the pertinent aspects of the revelation.

The special revelation requires special attention first. God has communicated rational, cognitive truth. He has not simply met man in an encounter. In this encounter He has actually mediated some word about Himself.[2]

The revelation has come through direct speech, in some cases. The testimony of the prophets in particular is that the word of the Lord has come to them, that God has spoken. Sometimes this came in a dream. At other times, it was via a vision (a conscious experience of seeing persons, objects, and events). Sometimes it apparently was an audible voice. At still other times, there seemingly was inward hearing of silent speech. In each of these forms, however, there was communication of truth from one mind to another, truth that could be verbalized, expressed, and recorded.

Man, of course, is of a much lower level of intelligence than is God. God, however, knowing perfectly the creature whom He has made, knows those aspects or elements of man's knowledge content that can be employed in the communication of His message. He selects from man's concepts those elements that bear an analogy to God's own knowledge of Himself. Because God presumably has direct access to the consciousness of man, He is able to control even the thoughts of the receiver of the revelation.[3]

God also has made Himself known through His acts. Through the historical events of redemptive history, God has demonstrated something of His nature and character. His power, His love, and the actions that He rewarded and those that He punished have given considerable indication of the nature and pleasure of God.

2.   Bernard Ramm, *Special Revelation and the Word of God* (Grand Rapids: Eerdmans Publishing Co., 1961), p. 149f.

3.   Ibid., p. 59f.

Finally, God has most fully revealed Himself by His coming, or His presence. The New Testament asserts that God did not simply remain afar off but that He actually entered into human earthly history. It claims that Jesus, being fully God, became man and lived among men. Those who observed Him were actually observing God, so that this was a rather direct knowledge of the love, righteousness, and other attributes of God.

This communication from God has been preserved. The writers of Scripture were under an influence of the Holy Spirit to the extent that the writings that they produced comprised the actual message God wished to have conveyed. Thus the Bible's content can be referred to as the Word of God and regarded as being as authoritative as if God Himself were personally present saying these things.

The problem of ethics is then, on this view, first a matter of hermeneutics, that is, of determining what God has revealed on any particular matter. This, of course, is not always easy or simple, and no pretense is made to the effect that it is. This maintains, however, that God does have an objective will relative to any given situation, and that difficulty in determining what that will is should not be confused with there not being any such will.

When one begins to examine the Bible, however, he encounters a strange situation. The Bible does not lay down a large number of specific statements about every particular problem. If the Bible did accomplish this, it would be far too bulky and unwieldy to use conveniently. It would constitute an entire library, rather than a book.

Further, some of the specific commands seem to be tied to a local cultural situation, which has so changed as to make the command scarcely applicable today. Here the legalist simply makes these commands universal. These apply to everyone, everywhere, and at all times. The legalist converts biblical commands into laws. The approach here will be different, however.

This method could be better described as being *principial*, rather than *legalistic*. The Bible is understood as giving principles. These are objective, based upon the nature and will of God. These principles may have different applications in different situations, but the principles themselves are fixed and objective.

Unlike the situationist who contends that it is a matter either of love or principles, the Bible pictures a both-and situation. Law or principle is seen as giving flesh and content to the formal factor, which is love.

Thus, for instance, Jesus indicated that those who truly loved Him would demonstrate this, keeping His commandments (John 14:21). Moreover, Jesus' teachings contain numerous commands, or at least instructions. A close examination of the Sermon on the Mount, for example, indicates that it is replete with directives. Although these are not always completely specific, they are quite definite. The situationist argues that these are offered as illustrations of the type of thing that love might do. When read in its context, however, the impression given seems to be that this is what love *will* do or what it *ought to do.*

Further, Paul's writings do not simply leave love vacuous and undefined. The famous love chapter (I Corinthians 13) spells out some of the characteristics of love. In this passage, considerably more content is given to love than is found in Fletcher's depiction. Love is longsuffering, kind, not jealous, not proud or self-seeking, not easily provoked, and not vindictive. Whereas these are still rather general in character, it would appear that there are principles which, if brought to bear upon specific situations, might well dictate specific courses of action.

Nor is love the only norm that Paul lays down. He speaks of it as one of the "fruits" produced by the Holy Spirit, but not the only one. Others include joy, peace, patience, kindness, goodness, faithfulness, gentleness and self-control (Galatians 5:22, 23, RSV).

In the situations where Paul dealt with problems in the churches, he appealed to certain rules as being implied by love. In Ephesians 4:25-32, for example, he prohibits lying (v. 25), sinful expression of apparently proper anger (v. 26), stealing (v. 28), and bitterness, wrath, and anger (v. 36). These seem to be the correlates of love. Similarly, in

I Corinthians 6:9 to 7:40, he deals with problems related to sex and lays down a number of exhortations and demands. Thus Eenigenberg summarizes aptly:

> The Bishop and his friends have declared that it is love or rules. The apostle seems to be saying that Christ is best served when love for him and other persons follows ways which God in his Word has approved for the good of all. Some of these ways say quite definitely what is permitted in sexual behavior, and what is not. This is how Christ and love are served.[4]

Basically, the principial approach described in this chapter will say that although love is the great motivating factor and central element in the law, it is not the only principle to be considered. It may be the formal principle, of which the law is the content.

A REVISED CLASSIFICATION
OF ETHICAL METHODOLOGIES

A new classification of ethical approaches is needed. Fletcher, it will be recalled, spoke of three types—the antinomian on the left and the legalistic on the right, with his own situationism occupying the entire territory in between. Rather, there ought to be two major designations of types of approach: objective and subjective. Within each of these there would be further breakdowns as follows:

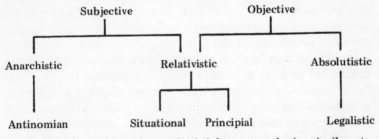

On this basis, the principial approach is similar to situationism in that the application of a principle depends

---

4. Elton M. Eenigenberg, "How New Is the New Morality?" *The Reformed Review* 20, no. 3 (March 1967): 22.

upon the set of circumstances involved in the situation under consideration. It differs, however, for the principles are objective, normative values. The difference between this method and legalism is that the application of the principle varies according to circumstances in this approach, whereas for legalism the principle actually is its application.

THE STATUS OF PRINCIPLES

At some points, the principles are so specifically spelled out as to be equatable with rule. Thus, one principle revealed in Scripture as apparently being esteemed and supported by God is the preservation of human life when possible. God is the one who has created and sustains life, and the maintenance of His creation is important. This seems to dictate a prohibition of murder, the voluntary, avoidable, unprovoked, and unnecessary killing of another person. Although these adjectives are sufficiently loose as to require considerable definition, the point is that instances of this type of action would always be wrong regardless of situation.[5] An action that does not fit this description would not constitute murder and would consequently not be wrong (at least on these grounds). Here the principle (preservation of human life) is embodied in a rather specific dictate (the prohibition of murder), which becomes a universal.

In other cases, the identification is not nearly so close, however. One divinely endorsed principle seems to be human modesty and the maintenance of an appearance of purity with the avoidance of appearance that would be associated with lack of chastity. The concrete form that this would take might vary greatly from one culture to another.

Paul, in I Corinthians 11:5, 6, commanded the women not to shave their hair. This, it appears, was an instance of application of the principle listed above, for in that place, shaven hair was the badge of the adulteress. Consequently, these Christian women were to avoid any appearance that

---

5. Charles E. Curran, "Dialogue With Joseph Fletcher," *The Homiletical and Pastoral Review* 67, no. 10 (July 1967): 823.

might be associated with immorality. There was nothing inherently wrong with short hair, but in that situation it was wrong. In another culture it might be long hair that had the same association, and there it would be wrong.

Some legalists (the more extreme type, which Fletcher generally accepts as his examples) would make Paul's command into a law to be universally obeyed regardless of circumstance. Short hair is always wrong, for all women, everywhere. The situationist would not admit of any universal principle except love, but has some difficulty determining just how this rather indefinite concept applies in a specific case without further elaboration.

THE PRINCIPIAL ROUTE
TO ETHICAL CONCLUSIONS

For the principial ethic, then, there are principles in addition to love that are objectively and universally valid. They hold regardless of situation. The form that their expression and application may take, however, will vary with the circumstances of the concrete situation. The task of the Christian ethicist will in this scheme involve several steps:

1. Determination of the relevant principles.
2. Combination of these to form some type of rules, or directives.
3. Refinement of the rules, from general or generic, to specific.
4. Determination of the application of these specific rules, or subsumption of cases to rules.
5. Deciding upon a method of disposition of cases that do not seem to be subsumable under any rule.

THE PROBLEM OF EXCEPTIONS

This is to say that specific rules do not admit of exceptions. There seem to be three ways of regarding apparent exceptions to general rules:

1. The exception is unique. There is something about the particular case under consideration that lifts it above the general rule. The case itself is so unique, however, that the

exception-making rule cannot be generalized or extended to other cases. It applies to this case, and to it alone.

2. There are certain exempting conditions that, when present, place a certain case outside of the realm of the proffered rule. This would mean that not only is a specific case to be regarded as an exception, but that the rule in question would not apply to *any* instance of this. Thus the rule "X is never right" does not hold in cases of Y.

3. The seeming exempting conditions are simply further specifications of the rule. On this basis, "X is never right" is a generic rule. It must be further refined into a specific rule. Thus, cases of Y are not exceptions to rule X. The rule applying to cases XY is a different rule than that pertaining to cases of XZ, although both belong to the same genus X.[6]

To cite the example used earlier, the principle of modesty when applied in a situation where short hair is the mark of an adulteress proscribes cutting of hair. In another cultural situation, where the opposite connotation was attached, the rule might be that hair should be cut. The more generic rule, that women ought not by their appearance to be associated with that which is morally improper, is not compromised by this. Nor is the general principle of modesty endangered.

There is, of course, a continuum, with principles of generality on one end, and concrete, particular directives (such as "Give that man that food, now!") on the other end. One cannot properly speak of the universalization of a particular command, since there is not, has never been, and will never be, another instance of this food, this man, and this moment. What is usually universalized is the most specific rule that can be formulated, short of the concrete directive.

But what of the problem of the case that is novel, or to which no formulated rule appears to apply? Here, the

---

6.   Paul Ramsey, "The Case of the Curious Exception," *Norm and Context in Christian Ethics*, ed. Gene H. Outka and Paul Ramsey (New York: Charles Scribner's Sons, 1968), pp. 84-93.

procedure is what Frederick S. Carney calls, "extension of a rule."[7] One seeks to find the cases that he knows how to subsume under rules, and then he determines which of these the present case most clearly resembles. He then treats this case as he would the other. In other words, he extends the rule from a case to which he knows the rule applies, to one very similar.

This approach maintains that law and love are not opposed. The earlier examination of situationism revealed that the concept of love in that ethical methodology was so vague and unspecified as to be virtually lacking in objective content. Every attempt to give some content to love was branded as "intrinsicalism," "legalism," or something of that type. The position being presented here is that love is the formal principle, and that the law is the content given to it. The law tells us what love really means by giving further delineations of it, thus showing various aspects of love. The law, as the embodiment of various principles of God's will and His nature, gives us a clearer indication of what the good and the right are.

THE CONFLICT OF NORMS

But what of the charge that there could in the very nature of things be at most only one universal or absolute norm? It will be recalled that Fletcher argued this point on the basis that in a situation in which two absolutes were in conflict or competition with one another, only one could be absolute, and the other would have to succumb. Does this not devastate the principle approach? Two possible solutions to such a dilemma, however, are logically conceivable.

There is first the possibility that if there are two or more normative rules, these never actually come into conflict or contradiction with one another. If behind the moral structure of the universe there is a God who has designed it

---

7. Frederick S. Carney, "Deciding in the Situation: What Is Required?" *McCormick Quarterly* 2 (January 1967). Reprinted in *Norm and Context in Christian Ethics.*

and sustains and guarantees it, then is it not possible that He has so ordered His creation that the normative principles never do conflict? To be sure, Fletcher is able to show cases where supposed absolute laws collide. Several observations need to be made in this connection, however. First, these are hypothetical cases for the most part. Perhaps these are never found in actual experience. Second, there may be an indication that some of the supposed absolutes are not actually that, or that these cases are not instances of what they are supposed to represent, and that more precise analysis and description would reveal this. Third, the tension among various principles may help to define them. If Aristotle was correct in maintaining that virtue is a mean between two extremes that are vices, then it may be the "competition" from one principle that keeps another from becoming an excess. Hence, it would not be the normative principles that conflict, but caricatures thereof.

The other possibility is that there is a hierarchy of principles. Thus, it may be most important that principle A be observed and value A maintained; slightly less so that principle B be followed; still less so with principle C; and so on. What may also be involved in the ethical apparatus are principles of precedence, or "rules of the road," on the basis of which one ought to give the ethical right-of-way to principle A over principle B. Fletcher speaks of this as the twists and involutions of moral theology, and as rules for breaking the rules.[8] This appears, however, to be an oversimplification of the situation. It would be more accurate to push beyond Fletcher's identification of rules and ask what the rules really are.

THE NATURE OF RULES

This means that the laws, or normative statements, if put down in codified form, would probably be quite complex and involved. The laws that Fletcher is attacking are quite general, simple, and abstract. If this latter is what moral laws

---

8.   Joseph Fletcher, *Situation Ethics*, p. 19.

were, I would probably join Fletcher in his opposition to them. The laws he speaks of are of the nature of "Do A;" "Do B;" "Do X;" "Don't do Y." When one is placed in a predicament where he must choose between doing A and doing B or where doing X necessarily involves doing Y as well, there is difficulty.

As maintained earlier, the principial approach would not simply say, "It is good to do A" and "It is good to do B." It would apply its principles of precedence to say, "One ought to do A, except when B is present, and C is not present." This would seem to go beyond the criticism that Fletcher raises. At the same time, it differs from Fletcher in insisting that when the principles are applied and a rule formulated, this rule is objectively valid, i.e., it *is* right to do this.

THE DOCTRINAL CONTEXT

Good and Right

The principial approach draws a distinction between "good" and "right." The good is an ideal, which may or may not be fully realizable. It is right, however, to do that which would most fully actualize the good. It would be wrong to do less than maximum good, if one could do more. This recognizes that there will be some cases in which the best that can be done falls far short of the ideal. The best option available will be the lesser of two evils (for this approach does believe in intrinsically good and intrinsically evil acts). Yet this action, although it cannot be unequivocally termed "good," is right in the sense that it is that which one ought to do.

The Brokenness of the World

This is to say that this approach attempts to recognize and acknowledge the brokenness of the world in which we now live. Whereas there is an ideal that God desires man to attain, the world as we now find it may be in such a state as to render that objective unattainable in practice. Thus God's will in the ultimate sense (W_1) would be the fully good. Yet

God's will (W_2) is that man should do what most nearly approximates that complete good.

For example, it may be God's will that no human life should ever have to be taken. This would be the good. Yet, given our world in which men are characterized by greed, avarice, hatred, and fear, I may find myself called upon to take the life of another to defend myself or to protect the lives of my children. It may, in this case, be God's will (W_2) that I kill this man. I cannot say that what I did was good, but I can hold that what I did was right. This is not intended to create a sense of guilt in me, but it should produce an intense feeling of regret that the world in which moral choices are made and executed is of this very imperfect character. The distinction between God's will (W_1) and (W_2) is an important one. For a Christian to discuss the morality of war, for instance, without observing this distinction, invites confusion.

Sin and the Fall

The principial approach thus takes sin very seriously, not merely in terms of individual acts of sin, but additionally in the sense of the whole radical corruption of humanity and society. In the case of this variety of principialism this is related to the concept of a fall. This author believes that although man came from the hand of God morally good and without sin, the fall of the first human pair led not only to their own sinfulness but also corrupted the moral standing and ability of the entire human race.

There are further results of this sin and fall doctrine, as well. One is that this method does not assume the moral ability and capability of man. Man is considered to be a fallen creature whose natural inclination is toward evil, not toward good. He does not easily practice *agape*, or even desire to. Even when he wants to love, he does not always do what he is resolved to do. There seems to be a moral "drag" or friction preventing him from carrying out his good intentions.

Regeneration

This principial ethic is not an ethic of the ability of men in general. It is a supernatural ethic. Man is able to do the good (approximately) and the right only by the supernatural enablement of God. This requires that regeneration come first.[9]

Paul indicated in his writings that when a man in faith accepts the atonement that Christ has made for him and commits himself to Jesus, his moral and spiritual nature is changed (II Corinthians 5:17). Jesus indicated the same thing when He told Nicodemus, "You must be born again" (John 3:3). This is not simply a transformation occasioned by a trauma and resulting from a powerful resolution to reform. Jesus said, "That which is born of the flesh is flesh, and that which is born of the Spirit is spirit" (John 3:6). It is a supernatural act of God, by which the basic orientation of the individual's life is changed.

This is not a finalistic and perfected matter, however. In actuality this is merely the beginning of a process, which continues throughout the believer's life. Much of the old self-centeredness, prejudice, and indifference remains. The supernatural character of the Christian ethical life consists in two factors. There is moral strength supplied for performing the individual acts of moral responsibility. There is also the progressive change of the individual's character (called sanctification), so that increasingly it becomes easier to love his fellowman, to obey God, and to resist temptation.

Even for the Christian, however, the ethical standard held forth by the Bible is an impossibility if attempted unaided. It is necessary for the Christian to repeatedly depend upon God for help. Study of the teachings of the Scriptures, prayer for guidance and strength, and persistent effort to do God's will are necessary.

----

9. C. Peter Wagner, "Is Love Enough?" *Eternity* 18, no. 2 (February 1967): 59.

The Community of Faith

The Christian ethic, as here envisioned, is also an ethic of the Christian community. There is the support of social reinforcement. There is also the instruction and correction of others, many of them more experienced than the person himself. There is the positive direct encouragement of others. Whereas this is an ethic for the individual Christian, it is not an individualistic ethic. If it is to be practiced successfully, it must be within the context of the believing and practicing Christian community.

The Work of the Holy Spirit

The key factor in this conception of the Christian life is the personal working of the Holy Spirit.[10] According to the teaching of Jesus, the Holy Spirit would come and dwell within the disciples (John 14:17), and their efforts would be energized by Him. In this mystical experience, which most Christians do not claim to be able to fully understand or explain, the Holy Spirit somehow has access to the very center of the moral activity of the person.

The Holy Spirit also illuminates the Christian's understanding. Jesus promised His disciples that when the Holy Spirit came, He would guide them into all truth (John 16:13). He also said that the Holy Spirit would take His (Jesus') words and bring to remembrance all that He had said. Further, Paul speaks of those who are led by the Spirit (Romans 8:14).

Herein is a combination of promises. The Holy Spirit gives understanding of the teachings of Jesus, and thus enables the hearer to know the application of these. Further, the guidance of the Holy Spirit relates to the ability to discern the nature of the circumstances and find the proper course of action.

---

10. Henlee H. Barnette, *The New Theology and Morality* (Philadelphia: The Westminster Press, 1967), pp. 48-49.

The Supreme Standard: Jesus Christ

In all this, Jesus is regarded as the supreme authority. This approach asserts that Jesus was fully God, and that in His teachings He gave completely authoritative and infallible instruction. This means that His teaching is not subject to criticism on the basis of any other principle, even *agape*. If the teaching or the actions of Jesus seem at some point to conflict with one's understanding of *agape*, then one's conception of *agape* is in need of correction, not Jesus. Thus, for instance, in the case of the woman who anointed Jesus with the costly ointment, this method would hold that Jesus was right in what He did, and that the disciples (and Fletcher) had a defective understanding of the nature and place of *agape*. The place of Jesus as example as well as teacher should not be minimized nor overlooked. Since He was God incarnate, His actions may be considered to be a revelation of God's nature and will.

THE NEED OF LAW

It is the corruption of man's nature that at least in part is the cause of objective rules or principles having to be formulated into laws or concrete commands. Sin in its basic essence is self-centeredness. Luther spoke of it as man being "curved in upon himself." Reinhold Niebuhr defined original sin as the tendency to be more concerned about one's self than to be embarrassed about one's undue claims.[11] Because of this, one's judgment of what is the loving and therefore the good thing to do is biased by this self-preference.

Who among us has not had disagreements with others (either arguments or differences of opinion)? And who of us does not think he has been right at least half the time? If, then, justice is regarded as equivalent to love and if one is to love his enemy-neighbor unless too many friend-neighbors are hurt, is it not likely that the bias in favor of oneself and derivatively those most closely associated with one, will put

---

11. Reinhold Niebuhr, *The Self and the Dramas of History* (London: Faber and Faber, 1956), p. 30.

the agapeic calculus askew?[12] It is not that one will consciously do what is contrary to what love would require. Rather, it is that his perception of love's proper content and application is distorted and obscured by sin's effect upon him.

Thus Paul speaks of the necessity of law. It is essential to restrain sin. Man simply is not capable, in the natural state, of wanting to love, of correctly defining love if he wants to do it, or of fulfilling it if he knows what it is and wants to do it. Simply to say "love!" is not enough for man in the fallen state.

Man, when originally created by God, is described as being "in the image and likeness of God." Although variously interpreted and explained, this is usually understood to have involved, at least in part, a moral capacity and something of likeness to the moral nature of God. The Bible also indicates, however, that this image has been damaged by sin.

The need for definite injunctions and instruction did not begin with the fall, however. Even in the Garden of Eden, God's will was expressed in definite commands and prohibitions. Apparently even in the state of innocence (which is different from moral maturity) Adam and Eve needed some more specific guidance than simply to practice love situationally.

There seems to be another reason for principles taking universal form. This may appear to be a case of the "thin edge of the wedge" argument, but it is different in several ways. Suppose one applies a situational approach to the issue of adultery and marital fidelity. When he takes the marriage vows he is actually saying, "I promise to faithfully love you only . . . that is, unless in a given case, *agape* would be better served by committing adultery." Yet, as Paul Ramsey observes, marriages and other relationships are generally built upon the assumption of the fidelity of a pledge. If one makes a promise of some kind to another, that other is likely to assume that the promise can be relied upon to be kept. If this

---

12. Eenigenberg, "How New Is the New Morality?" pp. 15, 23.

is not the meaning that the promiser attaches to the promise, he probably ought to issue a sort of caveat: "I always keep my promises . . . unless it is more agapeic not to do so." In the absence of such a disclaimer, the person addressed is likely to assume that a promise is a promise.[13]

A BIBLICAL CASE

A final consideration, however, will be the examination of a certain biblical passage sometimes appealed to as an instance of situationism. Is it indeed such, or does it accord better with the type of approach suggested in this chapter?

One of these frequently mentioned is the case of Rahab and the apparent deception that she practiced in connection with the visit of the Hebrew spies to Jericho, as described in Joshua 2. When the spies entered the city, word came to the king, who sent men to Rahab instructing her to bring out the men. She did two things: she hid them under stalks of flax on her roof, and she told the guards of Jericho that the spies had already left. Was this a case of Rahab lying because of the exigencies of the situation, in which love was better served by her act? In particular, if God approved her action (no indication of divine disapproval appears in the biblical account), does this mean that God is a situationist?

The situationist would no doubt analyze the account somewhat as follows. What Rahab did was to tell a lie. Nothing, including lying, is intrinsically either good or bad. Only love is intrinsically good, and only unlove (indifference) is intrinsically evil. This is seen clearly in this case. To have followed the legalistic dictum here would have meant telling the truth and revealing the location of the spies. This, however, would have been the less loving thing to do, for it would have resulted in their deaths. No legalist, she told the lie, and what she did was not the lesser of two evils. It was a positive good, for it more fully served *agape*.

The principial method would not make the judgment

---

13. Paul Ramsey, *Deeds and Rules in Christian Ethics* (New York: Charles Scribner's Sons, 1967), p. 225.

like this, however. It would begin by asking what the pertinent principles that God has revealed are. These would seem to include the following:

1. The glorification of God.
2. The attainment of His redemptive purpose for as many men as possible.
3. The preservation of human life.
4. The maintenance and development of God's creation.
5. The avoidance of pain and discomfort for God's creatures, particularly haman beings.
6. The representation of truth to others.
7. The maintenance of relationships of mutual trust among men.

As we approach the situation of Joshua 2, how are we to determine what factors are to be weighted most heavily? Principle 2 above is very much involved. The conquest and occupation of the promised land were part of God's plan for the preservation of His chosen nation, Israel. Israel, in turn, was not an end in itself, but was to be the agent through which the revelation of God's message of redemption would be given, and through which ultimately the Redeemer Himself would come. Thus, it might be argued that this end (of God's redemption) justified a means that some would consider to be bad (telling a lie). Closer scrutiny is necessary, however. We must define just what a lie is, and then inquire empirically whether any given event (in the case at hand, Rahab's declaration to the guards) is an instance of the prohibited lie.[14]

Both on biblical and experiential grounds, it would seem that the prohibited lie is not simply failure to speak with exact verbal correctness in every case. It is voluntarily and intentionally, and for one's own welfare, misrepresenting matters to a person to whom the truth is due. In view of

---

14. Ibid., p. 203.

this, one must seek out regarding the context as to what we really have.[15]

The Rahab incident was not a normal relationship in life. This was actually a case of warfare. Culturally, warfare is generally regarded as an extraordinary situation. It is recognized that the antagonists are just that. Special rules apply. The rules of the game of warfare are not necessarily the same as those that pertain in a family situation. The enemy is not one to whom exact verbal correctness is owed. Here the normal relationships of mutual trust within society have already placed her sympathy and allegiance with the Hebrews. Her own people were at this point her enemies. Her motivation was quite possibly not the glory of God or the forwarding of His plan but rather the preservation of the lives of herself and her family. Whereas the verbal untruth that she told may well have been motivated by concern for her own welfare, it was not told to someone to whom the truth was due under the prevailing circumstances.

That war indeed involves such factors can be seen by an example or two. I recall in history class in elementary school reading of a particular tactic employed by a General Thomas against the British during the Revolutionary War. Stationed near Boston with a limited number of soldiers, he found a piece of terrain admirably suited to his purposes. There was a high hill some distance from the British, surrounded by a long, low valley that the British were unable to observe.

---

15. Charles Curran notes that the real question is the definition of lying: "For example, some situationists show the absurdity of an absolute norm against lying. In certain situations it seems that man must tell a lie; for example, the captured soldier who is asked about vital information. However, the defenders of an absolute prohibition against lying can come to the same conclusions as situationists. It all depends how one defines a lie! If the malice of lying consists in the violation of my neighbor's right to truth and not in the conformity of the spoken word with my thought, then 'principleists' and situationists can agree on the question of truth telling in particular situations." "Dialogue With Joseph Fletcher," p. 829; cf. Paul Ramsey, *Deeds and Rules in Christian Ethics*, p. 37.

Thomas marched his soldiers over the hill. When they dropped out of sight in the valley, they marched back around and over the hill again. The British failed to realize that what appeared to be a massive army marching toward them was actually a relatively small number of men, each seen several times.[16]

What judgment shall be passed upon Thomas? Was he immoral in what He did? Do people rise up in moral indignation over his deliberate deception? On the contrary, within the context of his actions this is applauded as a wise and proper course of action. Similarly, no one condemns the use of camouflage. It is part of the "rules of the game." For a nation to sign a treaty, however, and then blatantly disregard the promise made therein (i.e., lie about what they will do) or misrepresent certain facts in the treaty is regarded as improper.

There are other parallel cases. Consider a football game in which the quarterback takes the snap from center and appears to hand the ball to the fullback. The fullback, bent over, clutching his arms around his abdomen, plunges into the line. Meanwhile, the quarterback, the ball hidden behind his hip, "bootlegs" around end with it. The fans, however, do not rise to their feet in protest over the deceptive activity of the two football players. This is simply accepted as normal and proper procedure in an athletic event. The opponent is not, within this context, one to whom complete openness and truthfulness is due..

The point of all of this is that these instances do not serve as evidence that lying is sometimes right, and lying as defined above may therefore also be justifiable. What the Rahab incident helps us to see is what type of untruthfulness is prohibited by the Bible, or under what conditions failure to speak the truth exhaustively and exclusively is a lie and therefore wrong.

Again we have a recognition that we live in a corrupted world, one in which the best that can be done is far from the

---

16. Andrew Hepburn, *Boston* (New York: Scholastic Book Services, 1966), p. 98.

ideal that might be hoped for. Ideally, no enemies would exist: all men would live in perfect brotherhood with one another. Under these conditions the ideal of complete verbal truthfulness could be practiced. In such situations, the ideal of never terminating a human life could be realized. There would not be killing in self-defense or in just war, for such occasions would not arise. Similarly, no force would ever have to be exerted in apprehending criminals, for there would be none. But an ethic to be practiced presently must be designed for the world that now is, not for the world that ought to be.

SUMMARY

Thus, the principial approach sketched above is seen to be located somewhere between the situationism of Fletcher and the approach that he identifies with legalism. It is casuistical, yet normative. It maintains that there are divinely revealed objective principles in addition to love. It does not simplistically identify these principles with rules, however. It insists that moral decisions come from seeking to determine what principles apply in a given case and what priority is to be given to each. It is here that empirical inquiry enters and here that matters of judgment are involved. And it is here that the moral agent must humbly ask his God for guidance and wisdom, a wisdom that God has promised:

> If any of you lacks wisdom, let him ask God who gives to all men generously and without reproaching, and it will be given him (James 1:5, RSV).

Bibliography

Allis, Oswald T. *The Five Books of Moses.* Philadelphia: Presbyterian and Reformed Publishing Co., 1949.

Archer, Gleason L. *A Survey of Old Testament Introduction.* Chicago: Moody Press, 1964.

Baier, Kurt. *The Moral Point of View.* Ithaca, New York: Cornell University Press, 1958.

Baillie, John. *The Idea of Revelation in Recent Thought.* New York: Columbia University Press, 1956.

——. *Invitation to Pilgrimage.* New York: Charles Scribner's Sons, 1942.

Barnett, Lincoln. *The Universe and Dr. Einstein.* New York: New American Library, 1952.

Barnette, Henlee H. *The New Theology and Morality.* Philadelphia: Westminster Press, 1967.

Barth, Karl. *The Doctrine of the Word of God, Prolegomena to Church Dogmatics.* Vol. I, Part 1. Edinburgh: T. and T. Clark, 1936.

Bennett, John C., Review in *Religious Education* 61 (November-December 1966): 482-483. Reprinted in *The Situation Ethics Debate* edited by Harvey Cox. Philadelphia: Westminster Press, 1968.

——, et. al. *Storm Over Ethics.* Philadelphia: United Church Press, 1967.

Boice, James M. "United Presbyterians: Dropping the Traditional." *Christianity Today* 14 (June 1970): 31-32.

Bonola, Roberto. *Non-Euclidean Geometry.* New York: Dover Publications, 1955.

Borowitz, Eugene B. *Choosing a Sex Ethic: A Jewish Inquiry.* New York: Schocken Books, 1970.

Bright, John. "Modern Study of Old Testament Literature." *The Bible and the Ancient Near East.* Essays in honor of William Foxwell Albright. Edited by G. Ernest Wright. Garden City, New York: Doubleday and Co., n.d.

Bruce, F. F. *The New Testament Documents.* Grand Rapids: Eerdmans Publishing Co., 1960.

Brunner, Heinrich Emil. *The Divine Imperative.* Philadelphia: Westminster Press, 1947.

——. *Our Faith.* New York: Charles Scribner's Sons, 1949.

——. *The Philosophy of Religion from the Standpoint of Protestant Theology.* New York: Charles Scribner's Sons, 1937.

——. *Revelation and Reason.* Philadelphia: The Westminster Press, 1946.

Bultmann, Rudolf and Kundsin, Karl. *Form Criticism.* New York: Harper & Row, 1962.

Carney, Frederick S. "Deciding in the Situation: What Is Required?" *McCormick Quarterly* 20 (January 1967): 3-15. Reprinted in *Norm and Context in Christian Ethics*, edited by Gene H. Outka and Paul Ramsey. New York: Charles Scribner's Sons, 1968.

Cassirer, Ernst. *An Essay on Man*. New Haven: Yale University Press, 1944.

Chandler, Russell. "Lutheran Sex Code: Covenant Above Contract." *Christianity Today* 14 (July 31, 1970): 32-33.

———. "Lutherans in America: Drawing Together or Pulling Apart?" *Christianity Today* 14 (July 17, 1970): 33-34.

Cox, Harvey. "Introduction and Perspective." *The Situation Ethics Debate*. Philadelphia: Westminster Press, 1968

Crombie, I. M. "Moral Principles." *Christian Ethics and Contemporary Philosophy*. Edited by Ian Ramsey. New York: Macmillan Co., 1968.

Cross, Wilford O. Review in *The Living Church* (May 22, 1966). Reprinted in *The Situation Ethics Debate*, edited by Harvey Cox. Philadelphia: Westminster Press, 1968.

———. "The Moral Revolution: An Analysis, Critique, and Appreciation." *The Anglican Theological Review* 48 (October 1966): 356-379. Reprinted in *The Situation Ethics Debate*, edited by Harvey Cox. Philadelphia: Westminster Press, 1969.

Curran, Charles E. "Absolute Norms in Moral Theology." *Norm and Context in Christian Ethics*, edited by Gene H. Outka and Paul Ramsey. New York: Charles Scribner's Sons, 1968.

———. *Contemporary Problems in Moral Theology*. Notre Dame, Ind.: Fides Publishers, 1970.

———. "Dialogue with Joseph Fletcher." *The Homiletic and Pastoral Review* 67 (July 1967): 821-829. Reprinted in *The Situation Ethics Debate*, edited by Harvey Cox. Philadelphia: Westminster Press, 1969.

———. Review of *Morality and Situation Ethics*, by Dietrich and Alice von Hildebrand. *Commonweal* 85 (January 1967): 429.

Curtis, S. J. *A Short History of Western Philosophy in the Middle Ages*. Westminster, Md.: Newman Press, 1950.

D'Arcy, Eric. *Human Acts: An Essay on Their Moral Evaluation*. Oxford, Eng.: Oxford University Press, 1963.

Damant, V. A. *Christian Sex Ethics*. New York: Harper & Row, 1963.

Dewey, John *Freedom and Culture*. New York: G. P. Putnam's Sons, 1939.

Eenigenberg, Elton M. "How New Is the New Morality?" *The Reformed Review* 20 (March 1967): 11-23. Reprinted in *The Situation Ethics Debate*, edited by Harvey Cox. Philadelphia: Westminster Press, 1969.

Evans, Donald. "Love, Situations, and Rules." *Norm and Context in Christian Ethics*, edited by Gene H. Outka and Paul Ramsey.

New York: Charles Scribner's Sons, 1968.

Fitch, Robert E. "The Protestant Sickness." *Religion in Life* 35 (1966): 498-503. Reprinted in *The Situation Ethics Debate*, edited by Harvey Cox. Philadelphia: Westminster Press, 1969.

Fletcher, Joseph. "Agreement and Disagreement." *Commonweal* 83 (1966): 437-439.

———. "Ethics and Unmarried Sex." *Moral Issues and Christian Response*, edited by Paul T. Jersild and Dale A. Johnson. New York: Holt, Rinehart & Winston, 1971.

———. "Love Is the Only Measure." *Commonweal* 83 (1966): 427-432.

———. *Moral Responsibility*. Philadelphia: Westminster Press, 1967.

———. *Morals and Medicine*. Princeton, N.J.: Princeton University Press, 1954.

———. "Reflection and Reply." *The Situation Ethics Debate*, edited by Harvey Cox. Philadelphia: Westminster Press, 1968.

———. *Situation Ethics*. Philadelphia: Westminster Press, 1966.

———. "What's in a Rule? A Situationist's View." *Norm and Context in Christian Ethics*, edited by Gene H. Outka and Paul Ramsey. New York: Charles Scribner's Sons, 1968.

———, and Wassmer, Thomas. *Hello, Lovers: An Invitation to Christian Ethics*, edited by William E. May. New York: World Publishing Co., 1970.

Frankena, William K. *Ethics.* Englewood Cliffs, N.J.: Prentice-Hall, 1963.

———. "Love and Principle in Christian Ethics." *Faith and Philosophy*, edited by Alvin Plantinga. Grand Rapids: Eerdmans Publishing Co., 1964.

———. "On Saying the Ethical Thing." *Proceeding and Address of the American Philosophical Association, 1965, 1966*. Vol. 39. Yellow Springs, Ohio: Antioch Press, 1966.

"Freedom of Choice Concerning Abortion." *Social Action* 28 (September 1971): 9-12.

Gardner, Martin. *Relativity for the Million.* New York: Macmillan Co., 1962.

Green, Joseph F. Review in the release of the Sunday School Board of the Southern Baptist Convention, February 1966. Reprinted in *The Situation Ethics Debate*, edited by Harvey Cox. Philadelphia: Westminster Press, 1968.

Gustafson, James M. "Christian Ethics." *Religion*, edited by Paul Ramsey. Englewood Cliffs, N.J.: Prentice-Hall, 1965.

———. "Context Versus Principles: A Misplaced Debate in Christian Ethics." *Harvard Theological Review* 58 (1965): 171-202.

———. "How Does Love Reign?" Review in *The Christian Century* 83 (May 1966): 654-655. Reprinted in *The Situation Ethics Debate*, edited by Harvey Cox. Philadelphia: Westminster Press, 1968.

————. "Moral Discernment in the Christian Life." *Norm and Context in Christian Ethics*, edited by Gene H. Outka and Paul Ramsey. New York: Charles Scribner's Sons, 1968.

————. "Responsibility and Utilitarianism." *Commonweal* 91 (October 1969): 140-141.

Haring, Bernard. "Dynamism and Continuity in a Personalistic Approach to Natural Law." *Norm and Context in Christian Ethics*, edited by Gene H. Outka and Paul Ramsey. New York: Charles Scribner's Sons, 1968.

Harrison, Everett F. *Introduction to the New Testament.* Grand Rapids: Eerdmans Publishing Co., 1964.

Henry, Carl F. H. *Christian Personal Ethics.* Grand Rapids: Eerdmans Publishing Co., 1957.

Herskovits, Melville J. *Man and His Works.* New York: Alfred A. Knopf, 1951.

————. "Some Further Comments on Cultural Relativism." *American Anthropologist* 60 (1958): 266-273.

Hiltner, Seward. Review in *Pastoral Psychology* 17 (May 1966): 54-56. Reprinted in *The Situation Ethics Debate*, edited by Harvey Cox. Philadelphia: Westminster Press, 1968.

Holbrook, Clyde A. "The Problem of Authority in Christian Ethics." *Journal of the American Academy of Religion* 37 (March 1969): 26-48.

Hordern, William. *The Case for a New Reformation Theology.* Philadelphia: Westminster Press, 1959.

————. *A Layman's Guide to Protestant Theology.* New York: Macmillan Co., 1968.

Jewett, Paul K. "The Relation of the Soul to the Fetus." *Christianity Today* 13 (November 8, 1968): 6-9.

Judd, Walter. "Congressman Judd Talks to Young People About Politcs." *United Evangelical Action* 20 (April 1961): 6-9.

Kasemann, Ernst. *Essays on New Testament Themes.* Naperville, Ill.: A. R. Allenson, 1964.

Kaufmann, Walter. *Existentialism for Dostoevsky to Sartre.* Cleveland: World Publishing Co., 1956.

Kenyon, Sir Frederic George. *Handbook to the Textual Criticism of the New Testament.* London: Macmillan Co., 1912.

Kierkegaard, Soren. *Concluding Unscientific Postscript.* Princeton, N.J.: Princeton University Press, 1941.

Kline, Morris. *Mathematics in Western Culture.* New York: Oxford University Press, 1953.

Kuhn, Helmut. "Existentialism." *A History of Pholosophical Systems*, edited by Vergilius Ferm. New York: The Philosophical Library, 1950.

Kuhn, Margaret E. "Female and Single—What Then?" *Church and Society* 60 (March-April 1970): 19-27.

Lachs, John. "Dogmatist in Disguise." The Christian Century 83 (1966):

1402-1405. Reprinted in *The Situation Ethics Debate*, edited by Harvey Cox. Philadelphia: Westminster Press, 1969.

Ladd, George. *The New Testament and Criticism*. Grand Rapids: Eerdmans Publishing Co., 1967.

Langford, Norman F. "Ethics In Cold Blood." *Presbyterian Life* 19 (April 15, 1966): 10-11. Reprinted in *The Situation Ethics Debate*, edited by Harvey Cox. Philadelphia: Westminster Press, 1968.

Lehmann, Paul. *Ethics in a Christian Context*. New York: Harper & Row, 1963.

———. Review in *Episcopal Theological School Bulletin* (September 1966). Reprinted in *The Situation Ethics Debate*, edited by Harvey Cox. Philadelphia: Westminster Press, 1968.

Lewis, H. D. "The Voice of Conscience and the Voice of God." *Christian Ethics and Contemporary Philosophy*, edited by Ian Ramsey. New York: Macmillan Co., 1966.

Little, David. "Calvin and the Prospects for a Christian Theory of Natural Law." *Norm and Context in Christian Ethics*, edited by Gene H. Outka and Paul Ramsey. New York: Charles Scribner's Sons, 1968.

Long, Edward LeRoy, Jr. "The History and Literature of 'The New Morality.'" *The Pittsburgh Perspective* 3 (September 1966): 4-17. Reprinted in *The Situation Ethics Debate*, edited by Harvey Cox. Philadelphia: Westminster Press, 1969.

Mach, Ernst. "Newton's Views of Time, Space, and Motion." *Readings in the Philosophy of Science*, edited by Herbert Feigl and May Brodbeck. New York: Appleton-Century-Crofts, 1953.

Mackay, Donald S. "Pragmatism." *A History of Philosophical Systems*, edited by Vergilius Ferm. New York: Philosophical Library, 1950.

Macquarrie, John. *Three Issues in Ethics*. New York: Harper & Row, 1970.

Mayo, Bernard. *Ethics and the Moral Life*. London: Macmillan Co., 1958.

McCabe, Herbert. "The Total Context," *Commonweal* 83 (1966): 439-440.

———. "The Validity of Absolutes." *Commonweal* 83 (1966): 432-437.

McCormick, Richard A. "Human Significance and Christian Significance." *Norm and Context in Christian Ethics*, edited by Gene H. Outka and Paul Ramsey. New York: Charles Scribner's Sons, 1968.

———. "Notes on Moral Theology." *Theological Studies* 27 (December 1966): 612-617. Reprinted in *The Situation Ethics Debate*, edited by Harvey Cox. Philadelphia: Westminster Press, 1969.

Meye, Robert P. "The New Testament and Birth Control." *Christianity*

Today 13 (November 8, 1968): 10-12.

Milhaven, John. G. "The Abortion Debate: An Epistemological Interpretation." *Theological Studies* 31 (March 1970): 106-124.

——. "Objective Moral Evaluation of Consequences." *Theological Studies* 32 (1971): 407-430.

——. Review in *Theological Studies* 27 (1966): 483-485. Reprinted in *The Situation Ethics Debate*, edited by Harvey Cox. Philadelphia: Westminster Press, 1968.

——. "Toward an Epistemology of Ethics." *Theological Studies* 27 (1966): 228-241. Reprinted in *Norm and Context in Christian Ethics*, edited by Gene H. Outka and Paul Ramsey. New York: Charles Scribner's Sons, 1968.

Miller, William Robert. Book review in *The New Republic* (September 3, 1966). Reprinted in *The Situation Ethics Debate*, edited by Harvey Cox. Philadelphia: Westminster Press, 1968.

Mitchell, Basil. "Ideals, Roles, and Rules." *Norm and Context in Christian Ethics*, edited by Gene H. Outka and Paul Ramsey. New York: Charles Scribner's Sons, 1968.

Moody, Howard. "Abortion: Woman's Right and Legal Problem." *Theology Today* 28 (October 1971): 337-346.

Moore, George Edward. *Principia Ethica.* Cambridge: Cambridge University Press, 1929.

Muelder, Walter G. *Moral Law in Christian Social Ethics.* Richmond, Va.: John Knox Press, 1966.

Murray, John. *Principles of Conduct.* Grand Rapids: Eerdmans Publishing Co., 1957.

Nelson, James B. "Contextualism and the Ethical Triad." *The McCormick Quarterly* 20 (January 1967): 104-116. Reprinted in *The Situation Ethics Debate*, edited by Harvey Cox. Philadelphia: Westminster Press, 1969.

Niebuhr, Reinhold. *The Self and the Dramas of History.* London: Faber and Faber, 1956.

Nielsen, Kai. "Some Remarks on the Independence of Morality From Religion." *Christian Ethics and Philosophy*, edited by Ian Ramsey. New York: Macmillan Co., 1966.

Nygren, Anders. *Agape and Eros.* London: S.P.C.K., 1957.

Nowell-Smith, P. H. "Morality: Religious and Secular." *Christian Ethics and Philosophy*, edited by Ian T. Ramsey. New York: Macmillan Co., 1966.

Oppenheimer, Helen. "Moral Choice and Divine Authority." *Christian Ethics and Contemporary Philosophy*, edited by Ian Ramsey. New York: Macmillan Co., 1966.

Outka, Gene H. "Character, Conduct, and the Love Commandment." *Norm and Context in Christian Ethics*, edited by Gene H. Outka and Paul Ramsey. New York: Charles Scribner's Sons, 1968.

Phillips, Dewi Z. "The Christian Concept of Love." *Christian Ethics and Philosophy*, Ian Ramsey, New York: Macmillan Co., 1966.
——. "God and Ought." *Christian Ethics and Contemporary Philosophy*, edited by Ian Ramsey. New York: Macmillan Co., 1966.
Pike, James A. *You and the New Morality*. New York: Harper & Row, 1967.
——. *Doing the Truth.* New York: Macmillan Co., 1965.
Plato, "Protagorus," *The Dialogues of Plato*. Vol. 1 Translated and edited by B. Jowett. New York: Random House, 1937.
——. *The Republic*. Translated by Benjamin Jowett. New York: Random House, 1937.
Poincare, Henri. "Non-Euclidean Geometries and the Non-Euclidean World." *Readings in the Philosophy of Science*, edited by Herbert Feigl and May Brodbeck. New York: Appleton-Century-Crofts, 1953.
Polanyi, Michael. *Personal Knowledge*. Chicago: University of Chicago Press, 1958.
"A Protestant Affirmation on the Control of Human Reproduction." *Christianity Today* 13 (November 8, 1968): 18-19.
Ramm, Bernard. *Special Revelation and the Word of God*. Grand Rapids: Eerdmans Publishing Co., 1961.
Ramsey, Ian T. "Moral Judgments and God's Command," *Christian Faith and Contemporary Philosophy*, edited by Ian Ramsey. New York: Macmillan Co., 1966.
——. "Towards a Rehabilitation of Natural Law." *Christian Ethics and Contemporary Philosophy*, edited by Ian Ramsey. New York: Macmillan Co., 1966.
Ramsey, Paul. *Basic Christian Ethics*. New York: Charles Scribner's Sons, 1950.
——. "The Case of the Curious Exception." *Norm and Context in Christian Ethics*, edited by Gene H. Outka and Paul Ramsey. New York: Charles Scribner's Sons, 1968.
——. *Deeds and Rules in Christian Ethics*. New York: Charles Scribner's Sons, 1967.
Redding, David A. *The New Immorality*. Westwood, N.J.: Fleming H. Revell Co., 1967.
Redlich, Basil. *Form Criticism*. New York: Charles Scribner's Sons, 1939.
Richardson, Herbert W. "Evolution of Virginity." *Church and Society* 60 (March-April 1970): 5-18.
Ridenour, Fritz. *It All Depends*. Glendale, Calif.: Gospel Light Publications, 1968.
Robertson, A. T. *An Introduction to the Textual Criticism of the New Testament*. Garden City, N.J.: Doubleday & Co., 1925.
Robinson, John A. T. *Christian Morals Today*. Philadelphia: Westminster Press, 1963.
——. *Honest to God*. Philadelphia: Westminster Press, 1963.

Roleder, George. *Book News Letter* of Augsburg Publishing House, June-July 1966. Reprinted in *The Situation Ethics Debate*, edited by Harvey Cox. Philadelphia: Westminster Press, 1968.

Rawls, John. "Two Concepts of Rules." *Philosophical Review* 64 (1955): 3-32.

Sartre, Jean-Paul. *Being and Nothingness*. Translated by Hazel E. Barnes. New York: Philosophical Library, 1956.

Seiffert, Harvey. "The Promise and Peril of Contextualism." *The Christian Advocate* 10 (December 29, 1966): 11-12. Reprinted in *The Situation Ethics Debate*, edited by Harvey Cox. Philadelphia: Westminster Press, 1969.

Sittler, Joseph. *The Structure of Christian Ethics*. Baton Rouge, La.: Louisiana State University Press, 1958.

Smith, Harmon L. Review in *The Duke Divinity School Review* 31 (Spring 1966): 145-53. Reprinted in *The Situation Ethics Debate*, edited by Harvey Cox. Philadelphia: Westminster Press, 1969.

Soe, N. H. "The Three 'Uses' of the Law." *Norm and Context in Christian Ethics*. Edited by Gene H. Outka and Paul Ramsey. New York: Charles Scribner's Sons, 1968.

"The Soft New Morality." Report of a speech by Gordon B. Blaine, *America* 115 (July 1966): 4.

Spitzer, Walter O., and Saylor, Carlyle, eds. *Birth Control and the Christian*. Wheaton, Ill.: Tyndale House, 1969.

Stablinski, Kim. "Homosexuality, What the Bible Does . . . And Does Not Say!" Brochure distributed by the Metropolitan Community Church, Huntington Park, California.

Star, Jack. "The Presbyterian Debate Over Sex." *Look*, Vol. 34, No. 16, 11 August 1970, pp. 54-60.

Swomley, John M., Jr. Review in *Fellowship* 33 (November 1966): 24-26. Reprinted in *The Situation Ethics Debate*, edited by Harvey Cox. Philadelphia: Westminster Press, 1969.

Temple, William. *Nature, Man, and God*. New York: Macmillan Co., 1949.

Thielicke, Helmut. *Theological Ethics*. Foundations, edited by William H. Lazareth, Vol. 1. Philadelphia: Fortress Press, 1966.

Treese, Robert L. "Homosexuality: A Contemporary View of the Biblical Perspective." Paper prepared for the consultation on Theology and the Homosexual, sponsored by the Glide Urban Center and the Council on Religion and the Homosexual in San Francisco, August 22-24, 1966.

Unsworth, Richard P. "Today's Expectations of Premarital and Marital Sexual Behavior." *Church and Society* 60 (March-April 1970): 28-35.

Vincent, M. O. "A Christian View of Contraception." *Christianity Today* 13 (November 8, 1969): 14-15.

Vivas, Eliseo. *The Moral Life and the Ethical Life*. Chicago: University of Chicago Press, 1950.

———. "Reiterations and Second Thoughts on Cultural Relativism." *Relativism and the Study of Man*, edited by Helmut Schoeck and James W. Wiggins. Princeton, N.J.: D. Van Nostrand Co., 1961.

Wagner, C. Peter. "Is Love Enough?" *Eternity* 18 (February 1967): 59. Reprinted in *The Situation Ethics Debate*, edited by Harvey Cox. Philadelphia: Westminster Press, 1969.

Walters, Orville S. "Contraceptives and the Single Person." *Christianity Today* 13 (November 8, 1968): 16-17.

Waltke, Bruce K. "The Old Testament and Birth Control." *Christianity Today* 13 (November 8, 1968): 3-6.

Wassmer, Thomas A. "Is Intrinsic Evil a Viable Term?" *Chicago Studies* 5 (1966): 307-314. Reprinted in *The Situation Ethics Debate*, edited by Harvey Cox. Philadelphia: Westminster Press, 1969.

Weiss, Vernon L. "Read Fletcher Aright!" Letter to the editor, *Christian Century* 83 (1966): 1542. Reprinted in *The Situation Ethics Debate*, edited by Harvey Cox. Philadelphia: Westminster Press, 1969.

Williams, J. Rodman. *Contemporary Existentialism and Christian Faith*. Englewood Cliffs, N.J.: Prentice-Hall, 1965.

Woods, George. "Situational Ethics." *Christian Ethics and Contemporary Philosophy*, edited by Ian Ramsey. New York: Macmillan Co., 1966.

Young, Edward J. *Introduction to the Old Testament*. Grand Rapids: Eerdmans Publishing Co., 1949.

Index
of Names and Subjects

Index
of Scripture References